ROAD TRIP

Everything You Want to Know
About Every Kind of Trip
For Your Youth Group

Micheal L. Selleck

Youth Specialties

ZondervanPublishingHouse
Grand Rapids, Michigan

Road Trip
Copyright © 1993 by Youth Specialties, Inc.

Youth Specialties Books, 1224 Greenfield Drive, El Cajon, California 92021, are published by Zondervan Publishing House, 5300 Patterson S.E., Grand Rapids, Michigan 49530

Library of Congress Cataloging in Publication Data

Selleck, Micheal L.
 Road Trip : everything you wanted to know about every kind of trip for your youth group / Micheal L. Selleck
   p. cm.
 ISBN 0-310-57511-7
 1. Church group work for youth. 2. Voyages and travel.
3. Youth–Travel. I. Title
BV4447.S435 1993
259' .23–dc20   93-13460
                   CIP

Edited by J. Cheri McLaughlin
Interior design and typography by Rogers Design & Associates
Cover designed by Michael Kern

Printed in the United States of America

93 94 95 96 97 /XX / 10 9 8 7 6 5 4 3 2 1

Zondervan/Youth Specialties Books

Professional Resources

Advanced Peer Counseling in Youth Groups
The Church and the American Teenager (Previously released as Growing Up in America)
Developing Student Leaders
Feeding Your Forgotten Soul
Great Fundraising Ideas for Youth Groups
Help! I'm a Volunteer Youth Worker!
High School Ministry
How to Recruit and Train Volunteer Youth Workers (Previously released as Unsung Heroes)
Junior High Ministry (Revised Edition)
The Ministry of Nurture
Organizing Your Youth Ministry
Peer Counseling in Youth Groups
Road Trip
The Youth Minister's Survival Guide
Youth Ministry Nuts and Bolts
The Youth Workers Promo Kit

Discussion Starter Resources

Amazing Tension Getters
Get 'Em Talking
High School TalkSheets
Hot Talks
Junior High TalkSheets
More High School TalkSheets
More Junior High TalkSheets
Option Plays
Parent Ministry TalkSheets
Teach 'Toons
Tension Getters
Tension Getters Two

Special Needs and Issues

The Complete Student Missions Handbook
Divorce Recovery for Teenagers
Ideas for Social Action
Rock Talk
Teaching the Truth About Sex
Up Close and Personal: How to Build Community in Your Youth Group

Youth Ministry Programming

Adventure Games
Creative Programming Ideas for Junior High Ministry
Creative Socials and Special Events
Good Clean Fun
Good Clean Fun, Volume 2
Great Games for City Kids
Great Ideas for Small Youth Groups
Greatest Skits on Earth
Greatest Skits on Earth, Volume 2
Holiday Ideas for Youth Groups (Revised Edition)
Junior High Game Nights
More Junior High Game Nights
On-Site: 40 On-Location Youth Programs
Play It! Great Games for Groups
Play It Again! More Great Games for Groups
Super Sketches for Youth Ministry
Teaching the Bible Creatively

4th-6th Grade Ministry

Attention Grabbers for 4th-6th Graders
4th-6th Grade TalkSheets
Great Games for 4th-6th Graders
How to Survive Middle School
Incredible Stories
More Attention Grabbers for 4th-6th Graders
More Great Games for 4th-6th Graders
More Quick and Easy Activities for 4th-6th Graders
Quick and Easy Activities for 4th-6th Graders

Clip Art

ArtSource™ Volume 1–Fantastic Activities
ArtSource™ Volume 2–Borders, Symbols, Holidays, and Attention Getters
ArtSource™ Volume 3–Sports
ArtSource™ Volume 4–Phrases and Verses
ArtSource™ Volume 5–Amazing Oddities and Appalling Images
ArtSource™ Volume 6–Spiritual Topics
Youth Specialties Clip Art Book
Youth Specialties Clip Art Book, Volume 2

Video

Next Time I Fall In Love Video Curriculum
Understanding Your Teenager Video Curriculum
Video Spots for Junior High Game Nights

Student Books

Going the Distance
Grow for It Journal
Next Time I Fall In Love
Next Time I Fall In Love Journal

To my loving wife
Christine

Regardless of how far away I went or for how long, she
was always there at the end of the experience.
It is with loving gratitude that I place her
at the beginning of this.

Table of Contents

PART TWO: GET SET!

PART THREE: GO!

Acknowledgments

A journey of a thousand miles begins with one step, says an old Chinese proverb. My first step in youth work was in 1970 when my father asked me to counsel at a senior high summer camp. Little did I know that this was the genesis of God's establishing the course of my adult life.

Although I'm certain my father was desperate for counselors that summer, I know he invited me on this road because he was confident of God's gifts in me. People who believe in your potential are powerful motivators. My life has been richly blessed by my wise and loving parents, who always went the extra mile for the good of the family.

I took another step on my journey with youths in 1976 when my brother invited me to be a counselor on a wilderness expedition. He kept after me with reminders that one day I would lead in his place. I learned so much from him that I can scarcely begin to tell it.

Both of my brothers, Dave and Jerry, have been good and godly traveling companions over the years. With all three of us and our father being ordained clergy, we've shared a lot of common road. Each of us has our own unique spiritual blessings, but none of us could have gotten where we are today without the others.

Just as race cars have pit crews and a pit boss to tweak and fine tune the vehicle in preparation for the race ahead, I have been worked on by Dr. Chuck Foster, currently at Candler School of Theology in Atlanta, Georgia. Dr. Foster taught me group life, Christian ministry, leadership development, insights on teenage behavior, and joy for living. He has been and continues to be a faithful and dedicated minister of God. I'm deeply indebted to him for his knowledge and the Christian witness of his grace-filled smile.

Among Chuck's students, two well-intentioned iconoclasts have become important members of my life's pit crew. Without the devoted prodding, faith, and insight of Dr. Edward Trimmer and Rev. Mac Kelly, all three of us would be less than what we are. God is not done with us yet, my friends.

Rev. Bob Cagle has played a key role in giving concrete direction in my life, my work, and the way I view youths. Bob has shown me that youths are real people—capable now, yet growing still. Providing arenas for youths to demonstrate competence today while guiding their future progress is a creative task that Bob has mastered and is able to pass on to others. Bob is the one who calls me off the road when the traffic gets heavy. He is a man of peace and incredible depth and wisdom.

Two very special youths in my life, my own children, Amy and Rick, have shaped the content of this book. For the past seven years, at least one of them has been on nearly every outing I've taken. Through their insights, corrections, and suggestions, I continue to learn, perfect, and develop not only my style as a youth worker, but my identity as a father.

Without the help of Dr. Charlie Shedd and Rob Williams, this project may have never been attempted. Rob has traveled with me on a number of adventures. Over long miles of pleasant conversation, he convinced me I had something worthwhile to share with other youth workers. Dr. Shedd helped me to get specific with the design and content of this volume. I shall forever be grateful.

To the hundreds of youths that may find their stories recounted in this guidebook: Thanks for the great moments, the hard lessons, the laughs, the worship, the songs, the prayers, and the trust afforded me throughout the journeys detailed here.

North Georgia Conference of the United Methodist Association of Youth Ministers has prayed for me, prodded me, and promised to buy a copy of whatever I turn out, if I'll only stop complaining about how much I have left to do. Thank you.

My thanks to Noel Becchetti, my editor on this project.

Closest to home, blessings to the volunteer youth staff of First United Methodist Church: Janine Faucher, my able associate; Carl and Ellyn Trinrude, Dave Bell, Jenny and Andy Richardson, Sharon Swaim, Rob Lowry, Sandra Kenney, Rod Metcalf, Kathy Maxwell, Ken Mauldin, Fred Smith, Martee Horne, Arlyn Hawley, Martha Braswell, H. A. Richards, Kelly Cole, Trevor Smith, Peggy Galis, Claire McMillan, all of whom have covered for me so I could devote time to this manuscript. It hasn't always been easy—for any of us—but you didn't quit, nor would you let me. Special appreciation to Linda and Leon Smith for their help. God is watching you!

God has chosen to nudge all of these people, and so many more, to nudge me. Each has responded to God's prodding by reaching out to this greying sojourner. My most sincere and humble praise goes out to our heavenly Creator, God—my strength, my rock, and my salvation—for choosing great folks to mold and direct me.

Selah.

Part One

GET READY!

*I*t is said that although a boat can correct its course any time during a cruise, it's wisest to establish the correct route when leaving the harbor. Few words apply as aptly to preparing for group travel. Though the most poorly planned trip can have amazing benefits, and the most spontaneous of adventures can yield incredible results, few things replace careful planning as a way of ensuring a safe, high-quality, and cost-effective group adventure.

Since no two trip planners work alike when preparing a journey, *Road Trip* puts together a blend of what seasoned trippers do. What many veterans have learned by trial and error is offered here without the frustration and bruises of the hard knocks. Practiced trippers may be interested in what other old hands do, and those newer to youth ministry trips will benefit by both the whys and the whats that follow.

Establishing an accurate course early saves grief later on. While there are many dead ends, plenty of rough roads, and few genuine freeways in trip preparation, certain direct routes can save days or weeks of frustration. A blueprint of what to do, and when, would be impossible since each group and trip is unique. The *sequence* of planning, however, is transferrable.

Read ahead—not with an eye for copying others, but to use their experiences as a launching pad for your own ideas and creative designs.

*F*inancial Planning

1

Chapter

Tearing down a vacant house for profit sounded like a great trip fundraiser for the senior high youth group. The kids' energy (with just enough destructive overtones) could earn them the $1,200 needed to fund their trip. When do we start? was their only question.

The contract was signed, and the kids worked like gangbusters for the first week. Then the "fun" parts were done. No more writing names in the drywall with sledgehammer blows. No tearing off the roof shingles and seeing how far they'd fly. All that remained was hot, dusty, slow, manual labor.

As the weeks marched by, the kids' amnesia level rose dramatically. They forgot where the house was, the times to work, and even cooled on the idea of the trip itself as options for easier fun developed. The house was never finished. The youth minister subcontracted the job for all of the revenue they would have received in the original contract.

This tale of woe vividly illustrates the challenges of tackling the financing of a youth trip. Exactly how do groups pay for the big trips that we all hear so much about? How is cash generated? How is it managed? Simply put, where's the money coming from? Groups generally pay for a trip in one of four ways:

self-financing, drawing on the sponsoring organization's budget, through income generated by fundraisers, or a blend of any of the above.

Self-Financed Trips

Costs of a self-financed trip are entirely covered out of the pockets of those going. One simply divides the total cost of the trip evenly between the persons that sign up. In one approach the leader plans a trip then finds enough youths willing to pay what it costs to go. The cost of a $1,500 trip, for example, distributed among ten people, costs each individual $150. A second approach begins with the number of interested youths, followed by a meeting with potential trippers to estimate how much each person could pay for a trip. Say ten kids can each put in $100—you know you've got to plan a trip for $1000 or less. Knowing specific dollar limits helps you plan realistic trip goals.

The self-financed trip has two things going for it: It's the easiest way to finance the event (no fundraising hassles or budget battles), and record keeping is a snap. The formula is simple—only two more youths and you'll break even; three and you're in black ink.

The downside of a self-financed trip is that it's the most expensive for the individual participant. This may mean that youths who want to go will not be able to because of the price. To ease the cost burden, you may want to consider using the next method of trip financing.

Budgeted Trips

Successful soliciting of budget committees for monies to cover trip costs requires advance planning. Presentation is eighty percent of getting a request granted. Clearly define to your organization's governing body both the costs and the objectives of your trip, using accurate and easily understood facts. Anticipate objections (practice on unbiased others to see what they think and where they suggest changes). Allow your kids to share in the presentation.

Although most churches are eager to assist youths in developing their discipleship and are willing to listen to proposals, don't test the waters by requesting funds for a ten-day beach trip. Elders are more likely to fund trips reflecting the priorities of their church—mission trips or church camps, for example.

If one hundred percent funding is out of the question, try for a portion—say fifty percent—to lower the costs to participants, who can secure the balance through self-financing and/or fundraisers.

Fundraising

Fundraising is often a second career for youth workers. In a church that is ruled by the philosophy that youths need to earn their own way, or where there is no budget for tripping, fundraising makes trips possible. Youths who raise money for specific activities learn to strive toward their goals as well as work together with peers.

The best fundraisers trade goods or services for cash and require little up front cash investment—a car wash, a concession stand at a park or ball game, work teams that clean windows or yards for cash. Other fundraisers may require a small amount of cash to begin with. Suppers may seem expensive, but if tickets are pre-sold little money is wasted on too much pre-purchased food. A friend of mine in Hartford, Michigan, organized his group to make and sell ready-to-freeze sub sandwiches. Using ready-made crusts and deli meats and cheeses, an afternoon was all he needed to make and deliver the goods.

Consignment sales is another lucrative method. With these fundraisers, youths sell someone else's goods. These are usually of two types: Either the youths solicit orders and receive only the goods they know are sold, or youths accept goods by the truck load, reserving the right to return what portions didn't sell. (Caution: **Do not** pay cash up front for goods that you must keep whether or not they sell.)

In Atlanta, different youth groups sell Christmas trees, pumpkins, wreaths, and other seasonal items. This way when the sales are past, the wholesaler picks up unsold goods; the kids are not accountable for what they don't sell. Professional fund raising companies offer catalogues of wrapping paper, candy, cookies, and posters. The kids fan out into neighborhoods to raise money. The only goods shipped are the ones that have been prepurchased.

A-thons

Pledge-based "-thons" are a category in themselves. Individuals in the group secure pledges from others on an incremental basis. For a rock-a-thon, youths receive pledges for every hour during which they rock in a chair without stopping. For a walk-a-thon, youths receive a pledged amount for every mile walked. The varieties are endless.

Pledge models based on service, like the free car wash, also work well. Youths secure pledges for each car to be washed on a given day. When that day arrives, the youths wash as many cars as they can—free! Then they collect the pledges.

I have two concerns regarding "-thons": the persons pledging generally receive no goods or services for their cash (people quickly tire of supporting the group in this way), and collecting the pledged money is uncomfortable (a twenty-five cent pledge per washed car magically turns into a thirty-five dollar debt).

Collecting pledges often lasts a lot longer than the excitement of the fundraiser.

Whether your group chooses to sell goods or services or to promote a "-thons", check with parents, governing bodies, and civic and school authorities to be sure no local ordinances are being violated. Good communication and shared involvement are key elements in fundraising. If these elements are missing, guess who ends up doing all the work?

Customized Fundraising

In any group some youths willingly work to raise money. For them it's fun. Other youths in the same group either don't have the time or the inclination for fundraising and don't need the extra cash. Custom fundraising can get you past this roadblock to planning. Let the interested youths raise money at their own pace and in amounts that suit their financial needs.

Take a candy bar sale, for example. Each case contains fifty candy bars to sell for one dollar each. Of every dollar, half goes to the candy company and half is credited to the person who sold it. All participants are free to sell as much, or as little, as they want. The highly motivated may go so far as to recruit others to sell for them, while those who loathe selling or aren't motivated by need can pass without guilt.

Keeping Accounts

Begin planning your fundraising strategy by asking, How can the money we generate help the most youths? You can break this question down into bite-sized questions:

- How much money needs to be raised by the group?

- How many kids will need help with the cost of this event?
- Do we want to encourage visitors and newcomers to participate, or is this trip for long-time members only?
- Are we raising money to reduce overall costs, or do we need a fundraiser for specific individuals who want (or need) to raise monies?

If it's decided that reducing the overall cost of an event for all participants is what's called for, say so. Communicating your intentions to the planners and workers of a group fundraiser reduces possible misunderstanding among participants. Tell them they are working in order to reduce the general cost of the total trip so all pay less individually. In this group-style fundraising model, no individual records are needed or kept.

A trip for ten kids costing $1,500 can be partially financed by a car wash raising $300 and a dinner raising $200. That leaves only $1000 to cover remaining costs. Each youth can go on the trip for $100 rather than $150. The key is letting everyone know how the proceeds are being applied.

A few youth groups still chart exact working times and allot proceeds according to an individual's hours. Although individualized record keeping is fair—only the workers benefit from the profits—it's not a biblical model. It can breed a negative atmosphere within the group. Workers judge each others' output and the comparative difficulty of their jobs. Resentment grows toward those who show up but talk rather than help. Add to this the possibility that new kids may join your trip when the fundraiser is nearly complete, and you could have trouble. Cultivate a genuine Christian mentality among the kids: All together in the name of Christ.

All of the Above

A blend of self-financing, using budgeted monies, and fundraising is the model followed by most groups. Self-finance and budgeted monies ease the initial burden; fundraisers then help the youths to come up with the balance. The latter also helps to promote the trip, create a team mentality, and increase commitment and sharing within the group.

What works for another group may not work for you, so let your group add its unique mark to any of the methods you choose. Think through the ramifications of your plans. Do you have enough time to plan a major fundraising project? Do you have the people power to pull it off? Will the parents, your board, and the kids themselves support the project? Will the amount of money you raise be worth the effort? Reviewing these questions helps your planning process and enables you to make the kids and adults a part of the process.

The best fundraising ideas are yet to be imagined, but several books offer many ideas for raising money, including *Great Fundraising Ideas for Youth Groups* by Kathy and David Lynn (Youth Specialties/Zondervan). Also, don't neglect the proven ideas of youth workers in your area.

*P*rojecting Your Costs

2

Chapter

Y ou've come up with a great idea for a summer canoe trip. Twenty excited kids have signed up, and you know this is going to be a life-changing week. The only question is, How much will all of this cost?

Projecting costs for a trip, especially when you're new to tripping, can seem overwhelming. Few things bring youth workers into a prayerful mood quicker than the words, "You're over budget". A poorly projected financial plan for a trip can be disastrous, but basic preparation, using a few simple tools, puts you on your way to a successful trip.

Learning to work with and live within a trip budget can be rough because life on the road is seldom predictable. A trip budget, however, helps keep you out of a financial ditch. Let's say, as an example, you've targeted $200 per night for motel costs on a three-night trip. The first night your motel costs $250. Consulting your budget, you recognize you're now $50 over budget and need to make adjustments to keep trip costs in line. Without a budget, you might not notice the financial trouble sneaking up on you until it's too late.

To recover that $50, find a motel on the next night that will put your group up for $150. By saving $50 on the second night, you balance your trip budget.

Without a budget you have to count money, check lists, agonize over details, and worry about incidentals. An evening's quick review of a written budget reveals all the information you need to relax and sleep.

Laying Out Your Budget

Because each trip is unique, no one budget model works every time. However, outlining the components of each trip's budget isn't as hard as it sounds, and it gets easier as you gain experience in tripping. Think through each segment of your upcoming trip. Imagine waking up and getting dressed. Where is that cup of coffee or tea going to come from? What about breakfast? Where? How long will it take to order and eat? How will you pay? Who will tip? How much? After breakfast, what then? And so on.

As you take your imaginary journey, create a category for every item you think of that will cost money. Some categories fit any trip—such as lodging. Experience teaches you which are standard categories. Other categories are specific to a given trip—such as a fee for a sleigh ride.

The following basic items are standard for every budget:

1. Lodging

This can be anything from fancy hotels to tents at a state park.

2. Food

How is your group going to eat? (Note: If each person pays individually for each meal, omit this item.)

3. Transportation

Bus rental, van mileage, air fare, public transportation (subways, trolleys, city buses).

4. Fuel	If the cost of your transportation doesn't include fuel (such as when you charter a bus), include it here as a separate item. Include costs for oil, fluids, and a contingency fund for possible repairs.
5. Program	This includes costs for guest speakers, literature, videos, games, and anything else related to the program of your event.
6. Admissions and other fees	This includes costs for tickets to amusements, admission fees, equipment rental (canoes, climbing gear), and so on.
7. Contingency costs	This line covers unforeseen expenses: lost wallets, medicine, tire repair, surprise parking fees, and so on.

Designing a good budget requires input from several trippers. The sample budget form on the following page is a guide for planning your customized budget.

Lightning Budget Planning Sheet

TRIP DESTINATION:_____

Total number of paying travelers x registration cost = _____

	Balance	Expense	Line Item

Net income = $ _____

$ _____ $ _____   . . . _____

$ _____ $ _____   . . . _____

$ _____ $ _____   . . . _____

$ _____ $ _____   . . . _____

$ _____ $ _____   . . . _____

$ _____ $ _____   . . . _____

$ _____ $ _____   . . . _____

$ _____ $ _____   . . . _____

$ _____ $ _____   . . . _____

$ _____ $ _____   . . . _____

$ _____ $ _____   . . . _____

$ _____ $ _____   . . . _____

$ _____ $ _____   . . . _____

$ _____ $ _____   . . . _____

$ _____ $ _____   . . . _____

$ _____ $ _____   . . . _____

$ _____ $ _____   . . . _____

$ _____ $ _____   . . . _____

$ _____

Begin with total income on top balance line. Subtract out first listed expense and put new subtotal on second balance line. Each time a subtraction is made, list what it is for and move new total down, ready for next subtraction. When balance equals $0, the budget is spent.

Controlling Your Costs: Transportation

Under shade at a highway rest area, I studied my small caravan. The church bus was pulling a trailer loaded with canoes, and of our two cars, one was pulling another gear-loaded trailer. My road-weary drivers were resting. I had sponsored a good trip and had worked hard to keep costs down.

I had just finished patting myself on the back when a huge charter bus pulled up. Out poured dozens of laughing, energized kids. I thought to myself, *That looks like an easy way to do a trip, but the cost has to be incredible.*

Just then a woman who looked like the youth worker clambered down the steps. Seeing me and my menagerie of vehicles, she ambled over for a chat. We soon discovered that we'd been on similar trips over a similar time frame. The only difference was that she charged a lower per person rate than I had. How could that be? I had cut corners, borrowed vehicles, scrounged for cheap lodging, and gotten volunteer drivers. She was riding in air-conditioned comfort. All her kids were together in one vehicle, and there were no maintenance headaches.

It was then I realized that not all things are as they appear. A group staying at a nice resort could be paying less, the same, or just pennies more than a group going the budget route. How? By checking all the options—knowing that rates change due to volume discounts, seasonal rates, competition, and much more.

Ultimately, knowing the reasons rates change isn't as important as knowing the big secret: Businesses have to pay their bills just like everyone else. If money is flowing in, deals are hard to come by. If money is tight, the edge is with the consumer. A business person realizes that some money is better than no money. Always check options, even if they seem far-fetched at the time. And always ask for any discounts in all facets of your budget building: transportation, lodging, and food.

The first step in choosing transportation is determining how many people will probably go on your trip. A charter bus for twelve kids is cost prohibitive, and the church van and two cars won't handle a group of eighty. Starting from group size, you can weigh your transportation options intelligently. (We'll discuss the finer points of estimating your group size in Chapter 7.)

Buses

Given a group of travelers large enough to fill it, a bus offers the best bet for community building while en route. You may choose from among several kinds of buses, but each requires a good, qualified driver.

☑ *Converted school buses* have their place in the world. Often for sale cheap, they can serve for years. Many churches own and maintain these buses. (Most states require a driver to have a special chauffeur's license to drive one.) A few other adults and I once drove a school bus from Michigan to Wyoming and back—long days, slow climbs up big hills, hard seats, and hot winds. Regardless, we made it there and back without incident. The old buses can get the job done, and I'll be the first to admit it.

Still, there's something scary about going cross-country in a vehicle that has spent its entire life stopping every half mile! They get a whopping four-to-six miles per gallon and come equipped with sticky vinyl seats and windows that pinch your fingers. These buses, designed to run slowly and generally never far from a maintenance barn, spell "breakdown" when used for highway travel or high-speed cruising for days without end.

When your own bus goes down, you quickly discover that few mechanics will work on a bus. If a mechanic can be found, parts become the next issue. Ever hear of a bus parts store? Sure, it's a regular engine, but then it's never the regular stuff that breaks down. Ye Olde School Bus can do the job, but short trips are better than long ones—and keep a major credit card handy.

☑ *Charter coaches* come with a bathroom, reclining seats, a professional driver, air shocks, air conditioning, and loads of luggage space. School buses do not. In 1992 charter buses cost between $2 and $2.10 per mile. A trip to the Big Splash Christian Weekend may be 400 miles—800 miles round trip. That means the cost for the bus will be about $1,600. Don't panic! If there are forty paying riders, each person pays $40 for round-trip transportation to the event. If I were to drive my car 400 miles each way, it would cost me close to $80 in gas alone. By chartering a bus, the cost is half that, but to every person.

The charter offers three other benefits that driving on your own doesn't:

- In case of a breakdown, it's the company's concern.
- In case of an accident, it's the company's concern.
- You can relax, mingle with the youths, enjoy the ride, and arrive refreshed and ready to go.

☑ *Chartered sleeper buses* eliminate your need for hotels on the road. Gone are the normal rows of seats; they're replaced with bench-and-table combinations, allowing for a radical transformation at night. Out come hidden boards, cushions are rearranged, and Voilá! The interior converts into a two-tier sleeping arrangement. Boys on one level and girls on the other.

There are two obvious benefits. Since the bus is driven at night while everyone sleeps, 400 miles roll painlessly by before the group awakes. Also, you have no hotel stops to arrange and pay for. In the mornings the driver generally stops at a campground or RV park that has shower facilities. Sleeper buses don't cost more than a regular charter, either. A company I called recently quoted $1.80 per mile for the winter of 1993. The drawback is that sleeper buses don't necessarily provide the most comfortable sleep you've ever known. Nonetheless, I've found that kids want to try them just for the novelty.

☑ *Leasing a bus* from a regional or national company or from an independent operator is another option. When contacting a bus company, keep these facts at hand:

- The date, time, and place of your departure.
- Your destinations and the time you'll spend at each destination.
- Your date of return.
- A rough estimate of the number traveling.

The bus company representatives will likely have questions of their own. They'll also need time to work up a price. They'll then call you back with their price and some ideas to bring the cost down in case it has come in too high. Be flexible; listen to their suggestions. On the other hand, don't let them sell you something you don't want.

When leasing a bus, check on these things before you sign a contract:

- Is the cost of the driver's housing and food included in the price? Ten nights of private motel rooms and three meals a day for a driver can add a good bit to the bottom-line cost.
- How many drivers will travel with the group? How many hours will each drive? Where and when will the driver changes be made?
- Who is responsible for extra days on the road in the event of a driver error or a breakdown? Most lease agreements are figured on a per mile basis. If the group travels more miles than planned, who pays? Most bus companies stick to the terms of the original agreement, but ask.
- Don't sign anything that has blank spaces where the miles should appear or where the cost should be.

Double-check with the company the week before (as well as the day before) the trip is scheduled to leave. A couple of quick phone calls are all it takes to be certain all is still in order.

Buses are great options if you have enough riders to offset the costs. If your bus costs $1,600, and you plan to charge each person $50 for transportation, your break-even point is thirty-two riders. Five riders less and you will have to chip in $250. Five riders more and you have a $250 surplus. You can use this surplus to defray other trip expenses.

When choosing your bus, call every company in your area. Ask what discounts are available. You may get a discount, for instance, if your group can meet the bus at the leasing company. By driving vans and cars to the bus company and parking them for a week, you may save more than it would cost you for them to drive the bus that short distance to you.

☑ *Finding a good driver* is worth the extra effort or expense it takes to search one out. Bus drivers are wonderful people as a rule. If they've been in the business for any length of time, it's because they like people and are used to spending time with them. Still, a little extra checking is always in order. It's worth a few extra dollars in phone calls to find another youth group that can recommend a driver and company by name. Good-natured drivers are worth their weight in gold; do some digging to find one. The worst horror stories about charter bus trips nearly always center around the driver assigned to the trip. If you can't get a recommendation, talk long and openly with the company about your expectations for the driver.

☑ *Tipping bus drivers* is always in good taste, especially if they've done a good job. While there's no magic formula, according to the drivers that I talked to, I use the following method. Consider the number of persons being served by the driver (let's say forty). Figure the number of days involved (lets say five). That means the driver has been working for forty persons for five days. A tip of $1 per person per day would be $200. That would represent the maximum tip. The minimum tip in my estimation is $.50 per person per day, which figures out to $100 total. The tip can be figured ahead of time and built into the cost of the event, or the tip can actually be collected on a daily basis as a way of letting the youths share in the support of a driver. The way you collect it or on what basis you figure it isn't as important as making sure that it gets done.

RVs and Other Vehicles
It was a two-day drive from home to the Boundary Waters of northern

Minnesota. My brother had done the trip before in an old school bus. This time he wanted to try something totally new—rent motor homes and go in luxury. He could save money by doing meals in the kitchens, kids would have room to stretch out, he could avoid costly hotel stops (sleeping boys outside the RVs and girls inside), and drivers could sleep in comfort between shifts at the wheel.

My brother found a leasing agency that would allow groups to rent motor homes—not an easy task. He rented two motor homes large enough to safely and comfortably accommodate his group. At that time in the state of Michigan, no special license was required to drive a group in a vehicle like this.

If you're expecting a disastrous punch line, I'll have to disappoint you. The RVs worked out well, having only two drawbacks. First, his kids seemed more divided than usual when they reached their destination. Each RV took on a family identity because of the home style of travel. On his next trip, he shuffled the kids between vehicles at various intervals to prevent the heavy bonding from taking place too soon. The second drawback was cost. In studying it later, he discovered that he could have chartered a bus for the same cost and not had to drive.

☑ *Motor homes*, now a common family possession (even among members of your church), often sit idle except during a few weeks of the year. Borrowing RVs may be a cost-effective option for tripping. If you choose to use RVs, make sure you and your drivers are familiar with the operation of the vehicles—how to run the septic and water tanks, how to check the oil and other fluids, and how to understand and use the other gadgets that may come in a vehicle like this. Pre-trip driving lessons are very beneficial and help to relax the owners of the borrowed RVs.

☑ *A minibus*, a blend of a motor home and a bus, has the large chassis of a motor home, but the body is a fiberglass box with huge windows all the way around. Its bus-like rows of seats accommodate up to twenty-six passengers. Larger than vans but not as expensive as RVs, minibuses get reasonably good gas mileage and provide spacious travel comfort. The only drawback is the time and expense of preparing a driver to pass the special certification required in most states.

☑ *Vans* come in many configurations. The customized types usually hold only seven people, the standard ones hold ten to twelve, and the big ones manage fifteen. Even with these payloads, they manage to get around fifteen miles to the gallon. They handle more like cars than buses or motor homes, making driving more natural and relaxing. While they lack significant luggage space, they're powerful enough to pull a small trailer that can carry all your luggage.

Vans aren't cheap, but they're much more affordable than motor homes and more useable and functional than buses. New ones are as low as $12,000 (stripped), and used ones that are loaded can be had for less. If your van breaks down on a trip, mechanics don't look at you like you're from outer space when you ask for some help. Best of all, vans can be rented from just about everywhere: car dealers, rental agencies, generous church people, and so on. Lease rates vary greatly, making comparison shopping essential. Be sure you clarify pick-up and drop-off times so you aren't overcharged. Divide the cost of the lease and gas by the number of riders to get a read on your expenses.

☑ *The family car* best suited my first youth "group" of two kids and me. We fit nicely into the front seat of my 1967 Buick and still had room to spare. With such a naturally available option, you might ask why we don't see more of them transporting groups. Basically, when a group is too large for one car, it's better to move up to a van so the group can travel together. Cars offer the best gas mileage, they're less taxing to drive, they fit into parking spaces nicely, and they're designed for passenger comfort. The primary drawback is that your group can quickly outgrow this option. As long as your group can fit safely into one car, use it.

Figuring Fuel Costs

Before figuring fuel costs, you must first determine your trip distances and modes of transportation. No matter how fast or slowly you travel, the average speed of any trip is fifty miles per hour, which includes time for food stops, rest stops, and traffic jams. (This does *not*, however, allow for time lost to break-downs.) If your trip covers mountainous regions, reduce your average speed to thirty miles per hour for the miles you drive in those regions.

A fifty-mile-per-hour speed means that a trip of 200 miles takes four hours, a trip of 1200 miles takes twenty-four hours, and so on. This also works the other way. If a trip from Atlanta to Washington, D.C., takes twelve hours, the estimated distance of a one-way trip is 600 miles. If I know that a trip from Atlanta to Orlando is 500 miles, I can estimate ten hours on the road to get there. To make this work, you need to know either the mileage or the travel time between two points. Any good travel atlas has maps and charts that show approximate mileage and driving times between major points in the United States. How long it takes you to get somewhere influences where you choose to go.

Once you know the mileage of where you're going and what vehicle you'll drive getting there, use the following simple formula to calculate fuel costs:

Total trip miles divided by **miles per gallon**
equals
Total gallons needed for trip.

Total gallons needed for trip multiplied by **cost per gallon of gas**
equals
Trip fuel costs.

To help you get an accurate cost estimate, determine average miles per gallon by the following: buses get five miles per gallon; motor homes get six miles per gallon; vans get fourteen miles per gallon; cars get eighteen miles per gallon.

A van trip of **1000 miles** divided by **fourteen miles per gallon**, for instance, rounds out to about **seventy-two gallons** of gas per van. To do the second calculation, estimate the current cost per gallon of gas. Use a high estimate, just to be safe. (The price is always highest wherever you stop. The lowest price is always the next station you see. It's a cosmic rule.) Then multiply the **total gallons needed for the trip** (72) by the **current cost per gallon of gas** ($1.20) to get **trip fuel costs** ($86.40), which you round up to the highest ten to allow for oil and such. The bottom line is, you'll need $90 for fuel for a trip of 1000 miles in a loaded van. If you have twelve paying riders in that van, your transportation costs will be $7.50 per person.

Airplanes
Kathy was flying her group from Atlanta to Denver for a long weekend on the ski slopes. The flight, scheduled to leave Atlanta at 8:30 a.m., would take just a few hours. What a way to go.

Getting a group off on time, however, takes a miracle. Considering the half-hour drive to the airport, the need to arrive an hour early for check-in, and the inevitable last minute mix-ups, she told the kids to show up at the church at 5:30 a.m. That meant the kids had to get up around 4:30 a.m. Also, to get a reduced rate on tickets, they changed planes in Chicago. When they landed in Denver, they gathered their luggage and proceeded to their ground transportation. Finally they boarded a shuttle for the two-hour drive to Winter Park. Upon arrival they had to find the lodging office and pick up their keys. It was exactly 4:30 p.m. when they plopped down on their beds—6:30 body-clock time. Their five-hour trip took approximately fourteen hours, and they felt every minute of it! Although flying can be a convenient alternative, it's not necessarily quick. Flying with a group costs a day of travel time each way.

☑ *Calculating the real costs of flying* requires that you compare the cost of the plane ticket with what you would have to spend during a road trip—three meals per day, one or two nights in a hotel, and 100 or more gallons of gas. If driving to a site takes two days and flying takes a few hours, a great deal can be saved. While the savings won't add up to the full purchase price of a plane ticket, the cost difference between driving and flying is certainly reduced. If arriving fresh and relaxed is important, air travel is a great option. (Unless sitting in a tiny seat 40,000 feet above ground for several hours makes you nervous, in which case you may arrive a wreck.) Limits on luggage allowed is also a cost you must consider.

☑ *Controlling costs* is a must to make flying an alternative. Tickets are expensive; great deals are difficult to come by and include significant restrictions on the timing and duration of your trip. Still, it's worth a try for a flexible group.

When checking on prices for flights, have the following information ready:

- Date of departure
- Place of departure
- Destination city

- The exact number flying
- Date of return

Always ask for current discounts. A ticket seller need not mention bargains. If checking flights and costs on your own doesn't appeal to you, contact a travel agent to do the footwork. For each ticket sold by a travel agency, it receives a commission paid by the airlines, based on that agency's overall sales. The commission is not added to your ticket price. (More on travel agents in Chapter 5.)

If you fly, plan with these tips in mind:

- Pack within the airline's specified limits on the size, weight, and number of bags allowed. Clearly explain the limitations of carryon luggage, especially for your first-timers.
- Plan how you'll get to the airport.
- If you must pay to park vehicles at the airport, figure in that cost.
- If the group is being dropped off, arrange for someone to pick them up at a certain time and place.
- Determine ahead of time how your group will travel when you arrive at your destination city (rental cars, shuttles, buses). Where will you connect with your transportation, and what does it look like?
- Make alternate plans in case a change of planes en route or a delay that causes you to miss a connection causes you to arrive late to your destination.
- Minimize the impact of lost luggage by bringing some essentials in carryons.

Plan to arrive at the airport ninety minutes prior to departure to check in and get settled at the gate. The larger the group, the longer it takes. Flights change, tickets get lost in the computer, and so on, ad nauseam. All that's usually needed to take care of these last-minute details is *time.* If you cut it too close, your options go downhill fast. Leave early, check in before the crowds show up, then sit back and relax. Many airlines provide a group check-in desk where luggage can be handled more efficiently. When traveling with a group, take advantage of any group procedures the airline offers.

To avoid the panic caused by a lost ticket, many leaders give the youths only the ticket they need that day, saving the return trip tickets in a safe place. The youths usually appreciate this preventive help. What if someone *does* lose a ticket, though? A new ticket must be arranged for. If you have enough time, go to the service desk of the airline to file a lost ticket form, or call the travel agent who arranged your flight. A good travel agent who is available to talk to the airline may be able to get a replacement ticket for a $25 service fee. If time is short, purchase a full-price ticket and sort out the whole deal later. Ticket agents at the airline desk do not deal with major problems. Rather, they confirm that every person boarding has a valid ticket, and if not, they sell them one.

Trains

Ah, the romantic sense of traveling the old-fashioned way, seeing the countryside slide by, settling into the gentle rocking beat, eating in the restaurant car, walking over the couplings. When traveling by train, the ride itself can be the highlight of the journey—at least for a while.

Coach class cars look similar to the inside of a school bus, with a bathroom at one end. Better arrangements take more money. Private rooms and sleepers call for cash to be paid up front. Even coach class is fairly expensive, though. The cost of the average ticket may still run well over $100 per individual. When checking prices, be sure to know your exact times, numbers, places, dates, and so on.

Trains aren't the fastest way to go, but they do keep on moving throughout the night. This means that lodging costs can be eliminated from the travel portion of the budget. While food in the restaurant car is generally good, it is expensive.

Traveling by train raises some of the same questions as flying. How will the group travel after arriving in the destination city? How will they get to and from the train station?

Boats

For groups within reasonable driving distance of large bodies of water, boat travel may not be only a luxury option. Larger boats come equipped with beds, kitchens, entertainment centers, motorized dinghies that can pull water skiers, snorkeling gear, sailboards, and much more. The price of the boat, its captain, and your food is all you'll need for a great outing.

☑ *Motorboats* can get you to your location in a hurry and come in every shape and size, equipped in every way imaginable. Just ask about what's available. Motorboats are complex machines, and big ones require an experienced pilot. They also use a lot of fuel. Be sure to find out if the cost of gas is included in the contract.

☑ *Sailboats* are slower than motor launches and require many hands to make them go. This means plenty of time on the water and offers your kids the chance to be part of the working crew. Kids commonly take shifts piloting the boat through the night, working sails, and the like. Big sailboats come equipped with small engines. When the wind dies down, sailboats move along under power, slow enough to allow youths to handle the big wheel. Sailboats can use both the motor and wind at the same time, taking advantage of whatever weather is available.

☑ *Charter boats* are available through chartering agencies—you'll find them listed in the back of any boating magazine at a local newsstand. Call several agencies near your desired destination and compare prices and options. A boat priced at $2000 for a week that sleeps ten may lack air conditioning, recreation gear, appliances, and other extras available on a higher-priced charter. You need to decide if the extras are worth the additional costs.

Big charter boats require a professional captain who occupies a bunk, eats group food, and stays with you the entire week. When getting prices, be sure to ask if the cost includes your captain. As of this writing, a reasonably priced captain costs $800 per week. Captains, like bus drivers, can make or break a trip. Not every old salt works well with youths, or with a Christian group. The best way to find a great captain is to quiz other groups that have had experience with charters. The next best way is to clarify your needs with the charter agency.

When the boat docks in a port, you must pay a docking fee. When traveling across international boundaries, you must also pay customs fees. The customs fee is a one-time cost; the docking fee is a daily expense. In the Bahamas, for example, the customs fee runs about $35. The daily docking fee, depending on the length of the boat, can run $40 and up per day. Your boat serves as both hotel and restaurant for your group. When docking at a resort marina, you are recognized as paying guests of the entire resort, allowing you access to the swimming pools, private beaches, and other facilities at the resort.

If groceries are not included in your charter agreement, purchase them before leaving your main port. Groceries and restaurants in remote docking points are expensive. Don't forget to bring paper products, napkins, towels, and other essentials—these sometimes-overlooked items are expensive away from the mainland. When planning a menu, keep in mind that complex meals require hours of slaving away in a kitchen the size of a shower stall. Simple meals prepared by rotating cooks and clean-up crews ease the burden.

Boat trips are great options and can be less expensive than bus trips to near-by locations. Don't overlook this possibility just because it seems too costly or exotic. Check it out.

Controlling Your Costs: Lodging

4

Chapter

It was my first group camping trip. I planned to lodge my small group at a commercial campground. Before I left home I phoned the campground manager for directions. He assured me that I couldn't miss the place; I needed only to look for the sign.

After driving nearly six hours to get to our destination, we spent another two hours looking for that campground. Kids can be particularly cruel when they're tired, hungry, and cramped. We finally found the sign for the campground—unlit and no bigger than a dinner napkin.

I drove in the entrance and located the manager's office. Since we were a tad (three hours) late, the office was dark, cold, and empty. My kids, their faces glued to the windows, peered at me like emaciated prisoners of war. I had to maintain my composure or the Caine Mutiny would be a mere footnote compared to what might happen next. I turned and smiled as if I'd planned it just that way. Certainly I could find the tent area on my own and settle up in the morning. I drove up and down the narrow roads, our headlights rudely intruding into other camper's nests. At last I found what must surely be the right place. Wide open space, healthy grass, and no other campers nearby.

No sooner had we gotten out than a curious thing began to happen. Kids and adults ambled down the road with lawn chairs and cameras. Our group was to be the evening's entertainment—the comedy show, "Setting Up Camp in the Dark." Laughter and snickers punctuated the occasional applause we received from our audience when we finished something. If you've never set up camp in the dark before, continue to avoid it.

As we unpacked the borrowed tents, we discovered that there were no directions for setting them up. After an hour of struggling with the tents, it became apparent that besides the missing directions, about one-third of the necessary tent poles were absent. I'm not sure what haunts me more, the sight of those sad little shelters we called home or the echoes of laughter from our studio audience. Into each of these very humble abodes clambered my kids, ready for a night's sleep.

Ah, but the joke was only beginning—rain began to fall. Pup tents, when taut and properly set up, shed water nicely; taut couldn't describe what we had. They proved to be perfect for catching and retaining water.

Our living cartoon had one last frame, which we discovered when morning finally arrived. I hadn't found the tent site area at all; I'd set up our little community in the middle of the dog run. All the green grass and no other tents—I should have guessed.

Perhaps it was helpful experiencing discomfort and chaos so early in my traveling career. Over the past twenty years, that single event has pushed me to examine thoroughly a variety of lodging options when planning a trip.

First Things First

Before your planning goes too far, share your trip ideas with your church members. An incredible number of people own condos, cottages, and such. Others know of people who do; some will even do a little checking for you. One church member in Georgia knows the owners of a chain of motels in Florida. When the youth minister told him that he wanted to take the youth group to Florida for a week of fun and sun, the man wanted to help out. In a matter of minutes and a few phone calls, he struck an economical deal for the group. Through word of mouth many other youth workers contacted this person. Everyone wins.

Newsletters, regular or special monthly meetings, or an evening supper meeting provide great scenarios for giving a brief spiel of what the youths are planning. Offer people the opportunity to help you with some information or ideas. A few minutes of checking right in your own backyard before you head out on a treasure hunt may be all it takes to uncover a gold mine.

In the event that you need to investigate beyond local-church resources, however, let's look at some of the lodging options available.

High-Priced Options

Although you may not be among those groups who can afford to book higher-priced lodging, it never hurts to check. The high road isn't always prohibitively expensive. At worst you'll confirm that it's unaffordable. On the other hand, you might discover top-notch digs at bargain rates.

☑ *Condominiums* often hold from six to twelve kids per condo and are generally blessed with two or more bathrooms. The units have living space apart from the bedrooms, they come with kitchens, and are located strategically—on the beach, on the slopes, near a resort. Most condo complexes include swimming pools, meeting rooms, and other conveniences.

On the other hand, condos are someone else's living space, complete with real furniture and easily damaged items. With so many kids in each unit, chaos takes on unique meanings. Finding complexes that take youth groups may require hunting. Large damage deposits are often required up front, and may take weeks or months to get back. The lack of privacy inherent in a condominium complex and the lifestyles of other renters (going to bed before 10:00, for instance) may affect your program plans.

☑ *Rental houses* exist primarily in tourist areas. People buy second homes, use them a few weeks each year, then rent them the rest of the time to cover the mortgage. Owners charge enough rent to cover the costs, but not so much that renters are scared away. When a management company fronts for an owner, it charges a fixed rent set by the owner. The company can't negotiate a rate with you without permission from the owners. Some, however, know the owners well enough to call them up and work a deal. Always try to negotiate a better price. If rentals are slow, something is better than nothing for most owners.

A rental house accommodates a large number of people. I regularly use a house on Pawley's Island in South Carolina that sleeps twenty-six in beds and more on the floor. That means everyone is together for meals, discussions, games, movies, study, and sleeping (girls upstairs and boys on the first floor). Having everyone together produces great group dynamics and keeps the cost reasonable. To cover the cost of a $600 weekend's lodging for twenty persons, each person pays $30. That's only $15 a night for a private home at a prime location.

Like condos, however, rental homes double as private residences and can be filled with breakable things. Abuse isn't always easily cleaned up. Rentals are usually in residential areas, which may cramp your program style, especially at 9:30 p.m. when the neighborhood beds down. Rental homes can be hard to find and usually require digging out the names of several management companies before you strike pay dirt.

Medium-Priced Options

If there aren't enough youths going on a trip to offset the high cost of the above options, don't panic. When a sweet deal isn't forthcoming, go to a medium-priced option: campgrounds, retreat centers, college dormitories, and the ubiquitous chain motels.

☑ *Camps*—whether church camps, Scout camps, or other group camps—can provide cost-effective lodging. A typical camp has several sleeping cabins (or one unit for boys and one for girls), a dining hall, and a lodge for recreation and meetings. The setting is usually rustic—no TVs or stereos to short-circuit talks and story telling. Campgrounds often have marked trails, woods, a lake or pond, as well as courts and fields for outdoor sports. Sharing the area with other groups is likely, but not always the case. Sharing camps may mean you can't get private access to recreation areas except on a rotation basis. Camps also tend to be away from other diversions. When the weather is fine, it's a plus; when the weather is rotten, it's a pain. Prices vary considerably, and there's rarely room for negotiation.

The greatest limitation to group camps is being locked into someone else's schedule. If you're into a great discussion and the dinner bell rings, you stop talking and go eat. If it's cold and rainy one afternoon and you want a cup of coffee, good luck! Many camp kitchens are off limits and locked until they begin serving. Food is usually fine, but it's similar to what youths eat every day at school, so be ready for complaints.

☑ *Campus dormitory* availability depends on the time of year, but it's always worth checking out. Dormitories, like motels, are set up to accommodate many occupants. There's a good ratio of bathrooms to beds, and the rooms can handle almost any punishment kids can dish out. The cost varies from motel-like rates to pennies on the dollar. I've paid $35 per room per night (still a great deal with four in a room), and I've paid $10 per room per night—a steal of a deal.

On the other hand, it's not surprising to find a room stripped of every light bulb. There are seldom linens, so sleeping bags and personal towels are required. Ask if the dormitory you're considering is among those that are fully staffed round the clock. Usually that service is figured into a higher per room cost. Sometimes a house parent in residence assists with petty problems that arise ("I locked myself out of the room!"). Other times no one is readily available after 5:00 p.m., let alone at midnight. You can get a security person to assist you, but hours may pass before you see one. Check carefully the level of security available. Is a key necessary to get into the building, or can anyone get in? Are the parking areas well lit? Are there dead bolts on the dorm room doors? In some respects dorm security is maintained by the simple fact of hundreds of people living in a building together. When you use a building in summer, however, those crowds may not be there. Check it out.

✓ *Motels*, available everywhere, can fit just about any pocketbook. They usually deal with any size group, and they never close the office. Separate rooms with limited bed space, however, can encourage cliques to form within a group. Also, privacy for group meetings is tough to find. Finally, unless you bring plenty of adults, whole rooms of youths are left to their own wiles for considerable lengths of time. We'll discuss the dynamics of hotel and motel stays in more detail in Chapter 19.

Low-Cost Options

Occasionally you're willing to sacrifice convenience for price. In most respects your ease of planning is the only thing compromised here. Some low-cost options make the best memories.

☑ *Private homes* offer youths the opportunity to share with new people for a few hours. If you have enough advance time to set up home stays, this is a great way to go.

To make private homes work, you need a contact person in the host city. It may take several phone calls to locate someone willing to set up housing for your group. Your contact needs to know your exact head count and the gender division of your group. Hosts are given options to house boys or girls, told if breakfast is part of the deal, and instructed at what time to return kids to the meeting site. Upon your arrival at a prearranged site, the names of host families are matched to persons in the group. Private homes are usually free, and many times you can get breakfast thrown in on the deal. Many youths enjoy meeting new folks and don't mind the adventurous nature of this style.

The elements that make this style special can also be its biggest liabilities. A young person's stay in a host home isn't always warm and joy-filled. Youth leaders tell of homes where kids slept on a couch with a pillow, where it was ninety-six degrees and air conditioning wasn't part of the package, where lights out was 8:00 p.m. I've had kids tell me of being left alone for hours, stranded with strange guests in the host's home, and having free access to alcohol and pornography. I've heard of breakfasts consisting of juice and leftover halloween candy. In defense of this style, I've never had a youth come away with more than a headache and a deep and abiding wish for better luck on the next night's stop.

Locating good contact people is getting tougher all the time. If you have done home locating for groups passing through your town, you know that it gets old fast. Consider offering your contact person compensation. If you have fifty youths to lodge, offer the contact person $3 per head to locate them in trustworthy settings. It's still a cheap night's lodging, and the job doesn't seem so thankless and dreary.

☑ *Churches* generally offer no-frills lodging—free floor space, no showers, no food, no TV, no nothing. Some churches are equipped with showers, locker rooms, cots, and gyms; others have little more than braided rugs on cement floors. If you choose this route, be sure your group knows what spartan lodging it's in for—and that there is little room for complaints.

It's easy for a group to leave a church worse for wear—the number one reason churches decline to entertain groups. If you find a congregation willing to house you, treat the building like the sacred place it is. Leave it a little better than you found it. Even if the lodging is free, offer to pay for the gas and electricity you used.

Beware that although all the doors may lock, some churches in older, rougher neighborhoods may require added security. While there is safety in daylight, nighttime's a different world. A friend of mine put up his group in a church one night, parking the bus in the lot next to the church. The next morning they discovered that the bus had been broken into, and most of their gear had been stolen. Ask the host church about the security of the neighborhood, especially at night.

☑ *Commercial campgrounds*, although easy to find and costing little, may be in dubious condition. There may be showers, but how many work? How clean is the facility? Public parks, campgrounds, and state parks are convenient, but available reservations during peak season are few. Some parks offer sites on a first come, first served basis; at other times or locations reservations must be made months in advance.

Commercial and public campgrounds often have ball fields, courts, swimming pools, and hiking trails. On the other hand, lack of privacy and early lights-out may test your program planning. Your campfire sing-along may share airtime with rowdy neighbors on the other side of the hedge, and bad weather puts a serious crimp in community life. Crowded showers with long waiting lines and breaking camp every day are obvious drawbacks. Also, depending on your perspective, the following may or may not be a liability—morning comes very early in campgrounds! 'Nuff said.

Estimating Your Reservation Needs

Estimating reservations is an art, borne of experience and lost dollars. The best hedge against lost deposits is gathering information. Every rental agency, hotel, beach house, or condo complex has a policy on cancellations and deposit refunds. Make sure you thoroughly understand this information and write it down.

Sometimes there's no way to get around paying cash for a deposit. This is frustrating, especially when you haven't even printed your brochure yet. Still, if you must make advance reservations, you hazard an educated guess and send the money. Better yet, plan farther ahead. Find out the last day you're allowed to change reservations and receive a refund. Well in advance of that date, put out all your publicity and promotion and require sign-ups with deposits.

Here's how to figure how many rooms to reserve. If you expect a group of thirty-six to stay in motel rooms housing four each, divide by four and reserve that many rooms—in this case nine. If you're considering condos, find out how many each unit sleeps (say up to eight per unit). Dividing 100 kids into groups of eight gives you 12.5 groups. Round off to the highest number, and ask for thirteen units. In information-gathering stages don't worry about what effect gender division will have on room assignments.

The problem with making reservations based on a rosy picture of attendance is that a deposit based on this number will be required soon after the first phone call. No deposit, no reservation. The more units reserved, the more money required to hold the booking. Some places take a check and merely hold it as a sign of good intent. At other places a credit card number holds reservations. Some locations want to hold your cash—a request worth negotiating. Ask the reservation clerk how he or she would handle this situation if in your shoes. Allow the clerk to help you figure out a compromise to this impasse. People generally want to help if given a genuine chance to do so.

(For details on how to secure condos, hotels, and motels, consult the Appendix.)

Controlling Your Costs: Food

5

Chapter

I was a silent partner on one two-week trip—just coming along as support. The driving portion was three days each way. Registration included the cost of food while we traveled. The trip leader planned to buy food along the way, and we'd prepare it at roadside rests. Our first lunch of bologna on white bread, washed down with red punch and seasoned with potato chips, revealed that the trip leader's idea of a good lunch wasn't the same as ours. A few kids ate with glee, most managed a little bit, but some refused to eat at all. He spent about $40 on food almost no one liked or wanted. Kids ended up spending their own money at the next gas stop to buy what they did want to eat.

Of all the issues trip leaders deal with, none is as trying as what, when, how much, and at what price to feed the troops. Most youth leaders can count on one hand the number of times everyone agreed on a place to eat. Even quiet kids threaten violent insurrection when the issue of food is raised. While total agreement is too much to expect, a little negotiating can produce peaceful compromise among the parties.

There are basically two ways to handle food for a youth trip: the leader buys for the group, or the individuals buy their own.

Carry Meals with You

The most cost-efficient as well as nutritional way to feed a group is to buy food in bulk and prepare it as you go. Although the nutritional value of fast food is improving, it doesn't match the quality of food you can prepare. In preparation for an extended backpacking trip, my wife and I spent the better part of three weeks buying, mixing, baking, and drying food. We bought in bulk and broke it down into family-size portions, using resealable freezer bags. Each meal was planned for maximum taste, nutrition, and portability. For example, in one bag we pre-mixed ingredients for pan-fried bread. To use it we just added water to the bag, mixed the batter, and portioned it out into the pan. Though it took several weeks of work and planning everything worked wonderfully.

Instead of prepackaging all the meals, try preparing only a few scattered meals or one meal a day. Breakfasts are easy to plan; many kids don't eat much that early in the day. Nutritional lunches such as sandwiches are also easy to plan for. Suppers, traditionally the big meal of the day, can be managed creatively. Try a casserole that can be precooked and frozen. They are easily packed and can feed many.

Many foods come packaged ideally for traveling—milk which doesn't require refrigeration, dehydrated everything, coffee in premeasured filter packs. It's not difficult finding foods that travel well and provide excellent eating even several days out.

The fuss factor of carrying meals with you nearly goes off the index, however. Besides advanced planning and preparation, the food needs to be packed and transported. Boxes and coolers take up space and require people to carry them about. Building team spirit around meal preparation can easily slip into drudgery, if not handled well. Needed are one or two food captains who know every item in the entire grocery schedule to oversee operations. If this isn't done, it's not uncommon for Monday's kitchen helpers to use Thursday's lunch ingredients. If saving money is worth the fuss factor, though, this is an excellent option.

Handing Back Cash

Early in my ministry with groups, I included the cost of road meals in the registration fee and handed out money at each meal. I took the time to put the cash allotted for each individual into little brown envelopes, one for each person for each meal. As the youths got off the bus, I gave them their food allowance.

This plan worked well. Not once did I have to "lend" youths money because they had packed their cash into now-inaccessible luggage. Each participant was guaranteed meal money regardless of his or her personal spending habits. This method also insured that each youth ate regularly. On the other hand, stuffing hundreds of little envelopes with cash was tedious. Keeping up with a box full of little envelopes stuffed full of cash during the entire trip was maddening. Also, I had the weighty responsibility of not losing the money. Other than these few concerns, this model worked fine. Still, I found myself pondering alternatives as I handed out envelope after envelope to responsible, mature senior highers. Then it struck me—let them handle their own food money.

They Buy Their Own

That this simple notion eluded me for several years still causes me to shake my head and wonder what I was thinking. This method lowers the registration costs for an event, which then covers only the actual expenses as they divide up evenly among all the participants. Light eaters spend their money in other ways;

heavy eaters pay their own way. The fuss factor is almost nonexistent. Youths are allowed the dignity of handling their own money on a trip, which can help teens learn how budgets work (and why they sometimes fail).

The strength of this model, though, can easily become its weakness. Even though all youths fully understand that road meals are their own responsibility, some youths are better money managers than others. Invariably, someone loses his wallet (which, by the way, is always "stolen"—no self-respecting teen ever loses anything). What isn't lost is poorly budgeted, and with four meals to go the cash is already gone. Or someone packed her money in the bottom of a suitcase stuffed in the back of the trailer. Each case requires attention from you and your staff, creating the dreaded fuss factor. (I carry contingency cash. Regardless of which model I use, I end up spending extra money for food.) Some days it may seem as if keeping all the money yourself would be easier, and indeed it may. Yet over the years I have grown to love this model and use it almost exclusively. It's the most efficient and simple way to handle meals on the road.

Using this method of kids paying their own way still has to be monitored, however. When kids run out of cash I've heard some leaders comment, "Let 'em go hungry! They'll learn to budget their money by listening to their stomach." Unfortunately, when youths don't eat regularly, the whole group is taxed. Hungry kids often get ornery and even hostile, fights break out, and feelings are hurt. Always take care that each youth eats regularly and well. Everyone feels better and is well prepared for challenges ahead.

When figuring the cost of an event using this method, all meals to be eaten on the road are left out of the factoring. Suppose fifty youths are going to New Mexico for a hiking event. The trip requires two travel days each way. Figure gas costs, hotels, everything except food. When announcing the cost of the event, say, "This trip will cost $150 and twelve road meals." The most common response or question is how much a youth should carry for road food. Reply with a high/low figure. By avoiding restaurants which charge for ambiance (which may mean eating fast food most of the time), most youths can eat breakfast for $3, lunch for $4, and supper for $5. Figure an extra $2 for gas stop colas and candy to get a low-ball figure of $15 a day. High is $20. Any youths eating more than $20 worth of food a day don't need to ask how much cash to bring; they'll know.

One of the challenges with this model is paying the check at a sit-down restaurant. If separate checks are allowed (a rare option these days) and each youth orders alone, there's no problem. Splitting the check once the menus are gone, including dividing up the tax and tip, can be bewildering. Besides the math dilemma, you have to collect the right amount from each youth at that table before they go to the bathrooms or spread out among the video games. Not only that, those who wait for the total invariably pull out a twenty dollar bill to pay for a $7.83 tab. For this reason each table needs a patient, cool customer to handle the ways and means of paying the check.

If a young, inexperienced group is preparing to leave on a journey in which all pay their own way, invite participants to a restaurant practice night. Plan a supper at someone's house, pricing the meals and writing up a check for each table. Then create games around figuring out the fifteen percent gratuity, dividing the check, and collecting money from each person. Give each person at a table a chance to play accountant. Assign others in the group to role play common challenges to the accountant—leaving during the collections, not paying attention, trying to change the subject at crucial times, paying with big bills.

Demonstrate the necessity for keeping ones and fives on hand for splitting checks.

However you choose to deal with meals en route, take care that everyone eats and eats well. Next to the amount of sleep teens get, their diet dictates their moods and endurance. To ensure healthy group life, it's important that both are as stable as possible.

$\mathcal{P}$aperwork

6

Chapter

Most of us plan a trip assuming that our journey will be without trouble or difficulty. Consequently, items like insurance papers, medical releases, and registration forms don't automatically come to mind. But the first time there's trouble, we realize how important paperwork is. Tending to this often dreaded yet crucial area of tripping makes your trip safe, well organized, and legal.

Vehicle Insurance and Licensing

Every state has unique and regularly modified requirements for insuring and licensing drivers of vehicles. Six months before your trip, call the appropriate licensing agency in your state to learn what is required to qualify the drivers of the vehicles being used. Taking certification tests and completing paperwork for a special license may take weeks, even months.

It's the same for insuring the vehicles and occupants. Call the agency that writes the policy covering the vehicles you'll use. Ask specific questions about responsibility in the event of a claim. Are the youths covered for injury? Does the policy cover lawsuits? Whose insurance covers collision repair? Is the driver the only one covered in the policy? The questions are endless because the policies are as different as the companies and people who write them.

Each vehicle needs insurance coverage that applies to group travel. Each passenger needs medical coverage. Each vehicle needs collision coverage, and other peoples' property needs to be protected in case of damage. Sometimes a special policy rider can be added that covers all the occupants for specific travel days. The cost of these riders is usually minimal, and the kind of policy you carry isn't as important as having one. Don't leave home without current, valid papers showing that coverage is paid up to date, and that your drivers hold appropriate and current licenses.

Vehicle Registration

The best reason to have current registration on hand is to please the inquiring police officer that just pulled you over. Even if you never exceed the speed limit, numerous situations require current registration. This past winter a youth worker's caravan funneled into an inspection lane in Michigan, where she had to show both her insurance papers and registration for every vehicle.

Registration is also needed in case of an accident or to trace your vehicle if it's stolen. Make a copy of the registration to keep on your person, in addition to the copy that you carry in the glove compartment. As a lawyer friend of mine says to me from time to time, "When you least expect it, expect it!" Keep the registration in a safe and handy location, and hope it's never needed.

Permission Slips

I was just getting off the roller coaster when several of my youths approached me, breathless and wide-eyed. I knew something was wrong. Two of my kids had gotten into a fight in one of the restaurants and had used the food from the salad bar to garnish each other and the walls of the establishment. They had been taken into custody, and park security was awaiting my arrival.

I was escorted to a part of the park I'd never seen before and was greeted by police, imposing office doors, computers, lots of cameras, and two very unhappy ninth graders. When I told them to call home and ask to be picked up, I discovered one of the two kids was A.W.O.L. from summer school. He'd been dropped off at school early, made the fifteen-block walk to the church to join our trip, without his parents' knowledge or permission. Imagine their surprise when they answered the phone. I learned that day to use permission slips on all trips, including day trips. It's mandatory practice when working with any group of kids under eighteen years of age.

IMPORTANT: Without fail have your permission form and all other pertinent forms reviewed by qualified legal counsel in your area before using them. Nowadays, this kind of double-checking is mandatory. It's worth the extra effort.

Medical Releases

Every youth and adult on every trip needs a medical release including the following information: the name of the person, the name of the agency or organization sponsoring the trip to whom the release is being given, a statement of authorization, medical insurance numbers, personal doctor phone number, home phone number, nearest kin phone number, whom to call if no one answers phone number, and a place for a notary public's signature. Each state has specific regulations that change frequently, so check them out yearly. Call a local hospital to question the staff medical lawyer regarding what to include in a medical release. No trip leader should ever travel without medical releases for each person.

In addition to a medical release, carry a medical information form for each tripper. These forms provide medical history, such as allergies, allergies to medications, current medications being taken, and last tetanus shot. Update medical health forms for each trip. Health information changes as a child grows. Consider keeping a file card on each youth, listing insurance numbers and pertinent phone numbers. This way a parent isn't forever filling out the same information for every trip. For each trip a parent must sign a dated permission for that particular event. Put the medical release and permission slips into a trip file; make one of your best adult volunteers responsible to keep this packet with them throughout the journey.

International trips require passports, current shots, visas, and more for each person. Create a file jacket for each participant to keep in your trip notebook. If you're considering an international adventure, contact the embassies, consul offices, and tourism offices of the countries you intend to visit. Find out their requirements for visas and customs and follow them to the letter. You can usually locate these addresses from a reputable travel agent guide book or from your local library.

Emergency Road Service

We'd started up the mountain with two vans and a trailer full of skiing equipment and luggage. As we began our slow assent, the snow began coming down a lot faster than we were going up. In a matter of fifteen minutes, the roads were slick—we began slowing down and losing traction. Fifty yards past a police officer who was putting chains on his rear tires, our vehicles began to slide back down the hill. We had no chains.

After slithering off to the side of the road, we asked the officer to call for a tow truck that would help us turn around and allow us to get off the mountain. The wrecker came in a matter of minutes and got us pointed down the hill. Next we waited for a plow and a sand spreader to come by and followed it safely down. The operator of that wrecker took $150 of my contingency money for that little task. I didn't have emergency road service coverage at that time, but I got it soon after!

This little piece of insurance is worth its weight in pure gold. For about $50 per year, an emergency road service policy covers bringing you gasoline, jumping your battery, towing you from anywhere to the nearest place of assistance, and more. Check to see if your insurance carrier offers a policy rider. If it doesn't, you can purchase a road policy from a national chain such as A.A.A. without changing your insurance carrier.

Rosters and Emergency Contacts

Place in each vehicle and in the hands of each parent sending a youth on the trip a list of each person traveling, including addresses and phone numbers. Parents who need to contact parents of other trippers for any reason will have a list ready to work from. Name one person as the emergency contact at home. This is the parent that all other parents call for schedule changes, trip updates, or other questions. You need to call only one person to cover the home front.

Mapping Out Your Trip

Without exception, place a marked map in each vehicle. It's not okay to say, "We'll get to St. Louis and ask for directions." Nothing frustrates drivers as much as not knowing where they are or where they're going. They have little patience for this kind of disorganization.

Mark photocopies of pertinent map sections with colored markers to guide drivers where they're to end up in the event of separation from the caravan. If you know ahead of time where everyone is staying that night, call the location for specific directions. Give the written directions to all drivers. Besides being a responsible thing to do, it's very impressive to find a destination as if you'd been there a hundred times before.

Developing a Time Line

Brainstorming with parents is the best way to kick off your travel planning. Let them be a part of deciding where their kids will go. Plan to flavor the journey with experiences they're eager for their teens to encounter. Next meet with your young people to choose which of the possible destinations they want to commit themselves to. Pass the ownership of the journey to them right from the start. Discuss with them what tasks need to be accomplished to make the trip happen. As interest grows in the following weeks, use that task list to involve those committed to going along in the pre-trip preparations—right down to costs, reservations, and packing lists. The following work sheet gives you one place to record some of these early planning decisions.

Destination Unknown

Parents Meeting   (date)_____

Possible destinations   _____   Cost of transportation   _____
                         _____   Gas   _____
                                                   Special activity costs   _____
Possible dates   _____
                         _____   Daily food costs   _____
                                                   Special equipment costs   _____
Cost range   _____
                         _____   Per person costs   _____
                                                   Deposit policy   _____
                                                   Publicity director   _____
                                                   Flier in mail   _____
Youth Meeting   (date)_____   Reservations to whom?   _____
Destination interest   _____   Letter to parents   _____
Date of choice   _____   Pre-trip meeting   _____
Estimate of attenders   _____   Packing lists   _____
Length of event   _____   Chaperones   _____
Planning helpers   _____
                         _____   Event theme?   _____
                         _____   Program leaders   _____
                         _____
Planning meeting date   _____   Maps   _____
                                                   Health forms   _____
                                                   Medical releases   _____
                                                   Permission slips   _____
Planning Meeting   (place)_____ Follow-up letter   _____
Lodging choice   _____   Evaluation forms   _____
Reservation?   _____   Time/date of departure   _____
Cost of lodging   _____   Time/date of return   _____
Reservation?   _____   Emergency contact   _____
Transportation choice   _____
Reservation?   _____   Spending $$ needed   _____

Deposits and Commitments

7

Chapter

During the first summer of my friend's tenure at a new church, he planned a trip from upstate New York to Williamsburg, Virginia, and then on to Virginia Beach. He wanted to try one of the sleeper buses. The bus rented for $3,500. If he packed the bus with thirty-five, the transportation portion would be $100 each. If he got only ten to sign up, however, the cost shot to $350 each. The trip was planned for July, but the bus had to be reserved in January with a hefty deposit. How could he know how many would actually show up? He went ahead with confidence that when the time came, the youths would come. He signed the contracts and sent in a $1000 deposit.

At first things looked good. With several weeks to go, he had nearly reached his break-even point. Just when he started breathing easy, the bottom fell out. One of the summer baseball teams began to advance in the tournament. Suddenly eleven youths canceled. With those eleven went others who couldn't stand the thought of the trip without them; they canceled as well. He ended up going with nineteen youths and lost his shirt along with the confidence of some influential people in the church.

Beyond Guesstimating

My friend's disastrous (and expensive) experience leads us to two fundamental questions you must address when calculating your projected attendance for a trip:

1. How do I anticipate how many will attend months ahead of time when reservations and deposits have to be made?
2. How do I make sure those who sign up are serious about attending and won't back out at the last minute?

Thoughtfully considering those questions eliminates the most commonly used and least reliable method of projecting attendance: guesstimating.

Over the years I've learned three rules of thumb to make sure you don't paint yourself into a corner:

- Never plan a trip without input from parents and youths.
- Start small and grow.
- The more people you need to attend, the more time you'll need to promote the event.

☑ *When everyone shares in the planning process*, the odds for success are greatly increased. Still, to borrow from St. Paul's seventh chapter of Romans, I find myself doing what I know I shouldn't be doing, and not doing what I know I should be doing. Instead of planning ahead and involving parents and kids, I do it myself at the last minute. The problem is, if I *plan* a trip without involving parents and kids, I can also count on *pulling off* the trip without their support.

☑ *By starting small*, you won't blow the entire year's budget on one event, and you develop youth leadership for future trips. Trips done for the first time (which I affectionately call shakedown trips) should be geared toward a small group.

One year some kids in a friend's youth group expressed interest in white water canoeing. With some books and a few experienced scouts, he developed a great shakedown trip on the north branch of the Flambeau River in Wisconsin. He didn't know the river, the facilities, the terrain, anything. To offset his inexperience, he planned for a group of only six. The trip worked wonderfully. The ones who went became vital recruiters for the next trip. The last time he did that wonderful river, he took thirty youths. He started with a small group that had shown specific interest. He worked with that core—teaching, leading, and helping them become effective helpers for another trip. If a trip is worth doing again, the word gets out, and the attendance roster will reflect that interest.

☑ *To develop solid attendance,* plan one month of advance publicity for each full day of an event. If I'm planning a three-day retreat, I put out publicity three months prior to the event. A ten-day trip to the Wind River Range in Wyoming requires ten months of advance publicity. If I'm planning a ten-day trip with only seven months to go, I'd better hustle. If there are only five months left, I'd better ask if this trip is worth doing. With less than three months, I'd better cancel.

Registrations may come for last-minute trips, but parental questioning of your organizational ability erodes confidence in you and can lead to your downfall. It takes time for parents to budget out extra cash for big-dollar trips. The more advance the notice, the better. The more parent/youth involvement in the planning process, the better.

Making Commitments Stick

Youth workers understand legitimate, last-minute cancellations for personal illness or family schedules. But people who cancel out at the last minute because they didn't feel like packing the night before frustrate trip leaders. I've had youths sign up and then not show up for just about every reason imaginable. One girl backed out because she didn't want to get off the phone with Mr. Possibility when it was time to meet at the church lot. Some kids sign up for an outing knowing full well that they'll be on vacation with their family for that whole month. They simply don't think when they sign up; they just want their name on the list. What can be done to generate maximum certainty that registrants will show up for the trip?

☑ *Require deposits with registrations.* Don't let kids sign up without paying some cash up front. Add punch to that by closing registrations after a certain date. Tell each registrant no cash is refunded within a set number of days prior to the event. Then take this policy seriously. Allowing people to jump aboard at the last moment undermines the purpose and integrity of the time lines. If people are allowed to register with just a promise to pay later, don't be surprised when they don't show up and prepaid costs for that seat are lost. Be careful.

Turning someone away because procedure wasn't followed can be overdone and often invites unnecessary confrontations with parents. Closing registrations several weeks in advance can get you over that hurdle. Use the intervening time to meet with parents and youths in well promoted predeparture sessions. Establish rules, roles, and agendas at these meetings. Each preplanning step sends a message that extras can't walk in at the last minute. This also clarifies who is and who isn't going with enough lead time for planners to make adjustments in cost and space.

☑ *Establish a clear refund policy.* Let's say your February ski trip to Colorado costs $600 per person, $100 of which is required with registration. You have twelve registrations when sign-ups close in September. (This locks in the number attending, preventing any stragglers from jumping on board.) The next installment of $175 is due at Halloween, another $175 at Thanksgiving, and the last $150 after the New Year. In this scenario all participants have fully paid six weeks prior to departure. How should you work refunds for this trip? Here is my suggestion.

- Cancellations prior to November receive a 100% refund. You have a good chance to fill that vacant seat with three-and-a-half months lead time.
- Cancellations prior to January receive a 50% refund ($100 + $175 + $175 = $450 divided by 1/2 = $225). At this later date, and with the extra pressure of Christmas, you may have difficulty filling that seat for full price. A taker might still be found, however, for a discounted fee of $375, which is what you still need to cover that space after paying out your refund.
- Cancellations after the beginning of January would receive no refunds. You have little chance of finding a taker just five weeks prior to the event.

This refund policy protects the trip budget, raises consciousness about the trip, and keeps enthusiasm high. When Mom and Dad have several hundred dollars on the line, paid out over months of less-painful installments, commitment seems to follow naturally.

☑ *Reserve the right to approve substitutes.* A friend of mine in Spartanburg, South Carolina, warns of a mistake he made. He once let a kid who canceled out on a trip at the last minute find a substitute to take his place. Although the person canceling was an active member of the youth group, the person who went in his place didn't have a clue what he was getting into. All week long the youth group put up with complaints like, "What's all this religious stuff?", "Why can't I smoke?" and so on. Inform your kids and their parents that they may only offer their seats to a substitute *after* they've submitted their selection to you and then to the youth group for consideration. Protecting the integrity of your youth group is an issue to be handled with careful attention.

Travel Agents and Other Professionals

Some trip leaders love searching for just the right location, setting, rate, and transportation for a trip. Others feel overwhelmed by the mere thought of wading through all the possibilities. If the details of your trip become too technical, or phoning for reservations makes you break out in hives, there's help.

As far-fetched as it seems, travel agents truly provide services at no out-of-pocket costs to you. Having been reared on sayings like "There's no free lunch," however, we're wary of those who say they can do our work and save us money at the same time. To understand how this works, you need to know how travel agencies function.

How Travel Agencies Function

A travel agency represents literally hundreds of travel and entertainment businesses all over the globe. Agencies serve as interpreters, helpers, reservation agents, and more. Unlike a retail store, however, which buys its goods wholesale and then resells them at a profit, travel agencies receive commissions from the airlines and resorts based on the bookings they make. Although some people believe otherwise, rarely are commissions added to the actual cost of the reservation. If you called Big Beach Resort and asked the price for a room, you'd be told the going rate (say $100 per night.) If a travel agent reserves that same room for you, the cost would still be $100 per night. The payoff for the travel agency that does your work is a small commission paid to them by Big Beach Resort. That small amount of money the resorts pay each time is offset by the increased bookings they get from having travel agents representing them to the general public.

Trip planners with enough ambition to sort through the thousands of possibilities might be able to put together a travel package more cheaply than a travel agent. Since resorts and airlines offer varied commission packages, an unethical agent could push the resort or airline that offers the best commission, even if it's not exactly what you need. Overall, though, reputable travel agents save you a big headache and a good deal of money.

Finding a Qualified Travel Agent

Word of mouth is the most reliable method for finding a good travel agent. And once you find one, you keep him or her for life, regardless of location. I know people in Georgia who still use agents as far away as Pennsylvania. Why? An ethical agent that understands and has a flair for individual needs, likes keeping costs in check, and keeps an eye out for packages that suit specific interests, is worth his or her weight in gold.

Ask your "frequent flyer" friends who their agent is. Visit the agent's office or call to see if you communicate effectively with each other. See if that person is someone you can ask questions of, think out loud with, someone who responds well to suggestions, will search out details, keep abreast of current discounts, and is sensitive to your needs. When contacting a travel agency, tell them up front that you're inquiring about group travel. Some agencies have a group travel specialist. If not, make sure your agent is willing to work with your kind of trip. An agent might even take a trip with you once to see just how you do things. Trust me, travel agents like to travel.

The benefits of having a travel agent in the group are numerous. On one trip, as we checked into a motel, we were billed at a higher rate than had been originally quoted. Normally it would take an hour or more to sort it all out—and even then I might still end up paying the higher price. This time, however, the travel agent who had set up the overnight stay was traveling with us. She stood at the desk for a few minutes, raised her voice only once, and when the dust cleared, we paid the lower quoted price. By that time I was already in the hot tub, relaxing and congratulating myself at having the foresight to invite my agent along.

Even if the booking agent is not traveling with your group, the agent and the desk clerk can fight the battle by phone. A travel agent is a natural ally whenever difficulty or confusion arises. The leisure industry can't afford to make travel agencies unhappy since they provide a major portion of their business. As your agent gets more familiar with your group's needs and preferences, he or she becomes more of an asset. Dozens of phone calls, contracts, confirmations, and clarifications are all taken care of for you as a matter of course.

Outfitters

A wilderness trip involves a great deal of planning because of the setting of the trip: wilderness. Appropriate equipment needs to be in good condition, routes well planned, permits acquired, canoes, paddles, life preservers, tents, lanterns, stoves, and food coordinated, vehicles arranged for drop off and pick up. An outfitter—an agent that equips a person or group for a specific experience—can do for you in the wilderness what a travel agent can do in civilization.

To understand what an outfitter does, imagine a wilderness canoe trip for ten people. After choosing a location, the group must be equipped for this special experience. Your options are to either collect, sort, and carry everything yourself, bring some stuff and rent the rest upon arrival, or hire an outfitter to do it all for you.

I've tried all three ways. Doing it all myself or supplementing various parts is cheaper. Being outfitted is better. I spent weeks coordinating the preparation of menus, purchasing groceries to be repacked in waterproof containers (washed out five-gallon pickle buckets), and making sure that each small group had enough of everything without having too much to carry. My older brother rounded up seaworthy canoes, hefty trailers, and suitable paddles and life preservers—a small nightmare. Getting tents, dutch ovens, maps, and determining the routes was more than we ever wanted to do again. The money we saved wasn't enough to justify the incredible amount of work involved.

An outfitter provides all the above and more. They can take a group of kids that arrive with only their personal clothes and put them on the water, totally ready for a wilderness experience. Because they are set up permanently in a specific area, they're ready with what you need, want, and must have. The price isn't cheap, but it's usually fair. With outfitters the old adage, "You get what you pay for," holds fairly true. Let me add a bit of hard-won wisdom. When entering a wilderness area with a group of youths, there's precious little margin for error. We hope for wonderful weather, no accidents, and flawless travel. In reality there can be a week of rain, broken bones, and significant risk. It takes no time to recognize equipment that isn't up to the test. Quality outfitters may cost a few dollars more, but their tents are waterproof, the food is plentiful, their permits are in order, their paddles don't break, and their first-aid kits are complete.

Like a good travel agent, a good outfitter takes the time to get to know your group. If one outfitter doesn't make you feel like your group is the key to their success, find another one that does. Word of mouth is the best reference.

When to Get Help

Taking a group on the road for a short trip requiring lodging for only a few nights may not seem worth bothering a travel agent for. I suggest letting them help anyway. Outfitting, though beyond the scope of this book, is also worth looking into. With both outfitters and travel agents, if something does go wrong, you've got a powerful ally ready to assist you in sorting out alternatives and answers. The little extra cost of an outfitter may seem unnecessary—until there's a problem. Then they're worth twice the price.

Part Two

GET SET!

Y ou've set your destination, figured your costs, worked out your promotion, and a group has responded with deposits and commitments. The big picture comes into focus. Now that the actual event is close, it's time to draw up plans for packing and transporting luggage, assigning rooms, and checking last-minute items. Come on— let's get set.

$\mathcal{P}$acking with Care

To be honest, I didn't realize that a trailer rented from a national chain wouldn't be waterproof. We'd driven for hours through a heavy rain. Finally at our destination, the rain had stopped—but the luggage was soaked clear through. Socks, sweatshirts, and T-shirts were all stained in fabulous arrays of tie-dye colors and patterns. Unfortunately, no one was into the tie-dye look. Examining our trailer, I discovered that some previous damage had opened a place for water to enter as it spun off the tires. It wasn't pretty, and the youths had a right to be upset. From that incident I began to give more care and thought to packing.

Individual Gear

You would think that the amount of luggage a traveler brings would be relative to the length of the trip. Not so. Unless guidelines are set, the volume of luggage is the same regardless of the length of the journey. Providing youths with a packing list is a must on any trip. Parents appreciate it, even if the kids never read it. Don't stop at the number of shirts and shoes, either; consider determining the size, type, and number of suitcases each person can bring. For example, if everyone packs a soft, midsize duffel bag, you can utilize under-seat storage in a van or a bus. On the other hand, if everyone packs a hard shell suitcase the size of a small piano, we're talking a big trailer.

I know a youth leader in Missouri who limits her kids to one hanging garment bag each. Clothing isn't hung in the bag as would normally be expected. Kids roll each individual item and pack it in the bag as it lays flat. When the youths show up with their gear, these garment bags stack neatly, one atop another. She claims to be able to pack for dozens of kids without resorting to a trailer. This also automatically limits how much each person brings, as only one bag is allowed per person.

Most youth workers allow each kid one bag to pack away and one to hang onto. In the personal bag they keep music, snacks, books, and so on.

Packing Blueprint
Giving specific directions for packing fits into four phases:

- What everyone *must* bring
- What everyone *should* bring
- What everyone *might want* to bring
- What to put all the stuff into

The *must* list includes things they'll need to be able to participate fully in the event: sleeping bags, towels, warm clothes, personal hygiene supplies, extra shoes, a Bible, and so on. The *should* list details things they can live without but would be helpful to have along: flashlights, spare socks, hats, and so on. The *might want* list could include cameras, binoculars, journals, guitars, and other things related to special interests. Tell youths what kind of container to pack in so they know ahead of time how much space they have to fill with items from the above lists. Luggage size and shape requirements keep luggage transportation under control.

Pack sleeping bags in waterproof, heavy-duty garbage bags with exterior identification. Waterproofing sleeping bags is preventive maintenance. Invariably, someone's shampoo bottle breaks open, turning someone else's unprotected sleeping bag into a wet, sudsy, cold mess.

Community Gear

Special materials for programs later on in the event, food, coolers, and firewood, are among the many items listed under necessary community gear. A youth worker from Louisiana uses big Rubbermaid tubs to pack the goods into. The tubs are waterproof, easily cleaned, fairly square for easy stacking, and easily numbered for identification. Coolers, a regular part of most trips, fit nicely in trailers or vehicles—serving as playing tables, leg rests, and with a little padding, nice beds for tired travelers.

Packing It In

If your vehicle has inside storage, secure the luggage to prevent it from falling forward in the event of sudden stops. One youth leader in Michigan told the following story about a packing fiasco:

"We piled all the luggage at the back of the school bus, taking the extra time to make sure it wouldn't slide forward. What we didn't do was consider that things could slide rearward. We had been on the road about an hour when the rear emergency door on the bus sprang open, spewing luggage all over the highway as we drove merrily along. If a passing motorist hadn't waved us down, we'd have lost a lot more than we did. We'd stacked the luggage so well from the front that we never noticed it was slipping out the back door piece by piece. We pulled over and made a mad dash to get as much as possible off the highway before it caused any accidents, or was made into luggage pancakes by some eighteen wheeler."

The types of vehicles you use and how many people you have going dictates how you'll handle packing. Charter buses provide loads of storage underneath the floor. Vans offer limited under-seat storage. An Atlanta youth worker suggests using the very back seat of a van for luggage if it's available. He observed that it forces the youths closer to the front, keeping them more involved in whatever planned activities happen as the miles roll away. I don't know what it is about the backseat of a fifteen-passenger van, but it encourages all sorts of curious activity. I'd suggest always filling the backseat up with something, if the seat's not needed for passengers, just to keep it empty of writhing, reclining youths.

Don't Leave Home Without...

10

Chapter

M ike!" the voice squawked at me from the citizen band radio, "We've got two vehicles in the ditch!"

I was leading a five-vehicle caravan to a retreat site in the hills of North Carolina. It was night, raining, and the roads were slick. In one motion I picked up the CB microphone and made a U-turn to the other side of the highway.

Again the voice crackled out, "Two in the median, but I think everyone's all right."

As I drove up to the scene I saw the two vehicles sitting dead center in the median, up to their axles in mud. One driver had been forced into the median by a truck that wouldn't move over when three lanes shrunk into two. The second vehicle, believe it or not, simply followed the other one right into the mud. We spent a hour or so getting the vehicles extracted and said a prayer of thanks that no one had been hurt. Pulling away from the scene, followed by the trailer and four other vehicles, I made a mental note of how valuable it was to have the CB radios along.

Whether it's an emergency situation or a matter of sharing information, CB's are worth the cost. Other items that a well-equipped group should have as it heads out on the road include a quality first-aid kit (and someone who knows how to use it), a fire extinguisher, a good spare tire and a working jack, a tool box, and (my personal favorite) duct tape. Different regions and seasons call for specialized items, such as tire chains for January mountain trips.

Citizen Band Radios

Communicating between vehicles can provide a frenzied challenge. I've seen groups converse with elaborate hand signals, headlight codes, marker boards in windows, signs, and much more. Nearly all youth trip leaders agree, however, that the most effective way to communicate is the CB radio. The installed types are mounted somewhere around the driver, hard wired into the fuse box, and have permanent mounted antennas. The other popular option, the portable models, plug into the cigarette lighter, have magnetically mounted antennas, and work very well. All the vehicles tune into the same channel, offering instant communication for the duration of the drive.

Even if your group travels in one vehicle, I recommend carrying a CB for emergencies. If a separate radio can't be arranged for each vehicle in your caravan, at least get them for your front and rear vehicles.

First-Aid Kits

While your vehicle first-aid kit doesn't have to be as complete as a wilderness camping kit, be prepared for cuts and scrapes, headaches and cramps, motion sickness, sprained limbs, and fevers. Replenish the kit before each trip and store it in an accessible location.

Aspirin and aspirin-free pain relievers are helpful, but don't give them out too readily. Help your kids discover and alter behavior that might bring on the headaches before letting them self-medicate. Motion sickness creates tension for the person stricken as well as the other passengers. Try moving motion sick kids closer to the front of the vehicle and telling them to close their eyes for awhile. If that doesn't work, give them an over-the-counter remedy, as long as their medical release doesn't restrict it. For the remainder of the trip, give the kids who need the medication their tablets at least one half hour prior to departure each day.

A bottle of hydrogen peroxide cleans cuts and scrapes and isn't as caustic as alcohol wipes, which are nonetheless good to keep on hand for the times when bubbling peroxide isn't enough to clean a wound. Include in your kit several sizes of sterile gauze pads and tape. Butterfly bandages are handy in the event of a deep cut. A butterfly holds things together until stitches can be administered by a physician. A few elastic bandages are handy for wrapping a twisted ankle or knee. Along with a working thermometer, keep in a plastic bag a dry washcloth to dampen with cool water to wipe the face and hands of a fevered person. While it doesn't do much to relieve fever, it feels wonderful. You may include other odds and ends in your first-aid kit. Don't try to be exhaustive; just put together a functional kit.

Fire Extinguisher

Equip every vehicle with a small fire extinguisher. A year before I arrived at my present church, a van full of kids experienced a van fire. They had no extinguisher on board; fortunately, they got out before the entire van went up in flames. Though we still laugh when we hear stories about that incident, it wouldn't be funny if someone had been hurt. An engine fire doesn't happen every day, but one time is all it takes to endanger kids. Be prepared.

Spare Tire, Jack, Belts, Jumper Cables

Carrying a spare and a jack seems so obvious it hardly warrants mention. On the other hand, when was the last time you took the spare tire out to inspect it and check its pressure? When did you last test the jack? Do your drivers even know how to change a tire?

How about replacement belts for the engine? Finding a mechanic that will change a belt on a weekend isn't terribly difficult. Finding the right belt *is* difficult. Carry the correct belts on board. Remember jumper cables, too. Like belts, finding someone who knows how to use them isn't difficult; finding someone who has a set could be.

Tool Box and Duct Tape

I never took this category seriously until I started traveling with Rob. Rob takes his old beat-up wooden tool box whenever he travels. When he pulls into the parking lot, he moves the box from his trunk to the vehicle the group takes. Inside the box is a big pipe wrench, a smaller crescent wrench, a full set of screwdrivers, a hammer, pliers, a voltage meter, wire clippers, wire, and a host of other odds and ends. I was most fascinated, however, by his inclusion of a big roll of grey duct tape.

After several experiences in which duct tape was strategic to the continuing success of our trip, I recommend this material be inducted into some sort of "great stuff" hall of fame. Once I used duct tape to repair a canoe that was wrapped around a rock in a rapids on the Flambeau River. When we pulled that canoe back into shape there were cracks at the water line on both sides of the aluminum. A few minutes with some heat and this magic silver tape readied that canoe to make the rest of the trip high and dry.

And Keep It Clean

I have a zealous associate that helps me prepare the vans whenever a trip is about to depart. She always packs a few garbage bags in each vehicle to corral litter while en route—a preparation well worth the small expense. If you forget them, pull over and buy some at the first store you see when you head out of the church parking lot. Believe me, you'll thank me later.

Group Dynamics and Room Assignments

11

Chapter

Awkward silence greeted my plea for organization. Already at this first overnight planning meeting preparing for a two-week summer missions trip, personalities began to show. Three of the kids were competing for "most obnoxious," two outgoing kids were asking and answering their own questions as several other kids observed in silence, friends were pairing off or trying to find out where everyone would be sleeping and what time breakfast would be. What was happening as the kids interacted fits loosely under the title of group dynamics—how groups develop and grow, how they interrelate, and how they deal with difficulties. Managing group dynamics is important to the success of your trip.

As a newly formed group coalesces, it runs what some call nonverbal group elections in which the group subconsciously elects persons to various "offices." The three obnoxious kids, for example, were running for most witty. Eventually, one was awarded that title and became known as the group clown. The two he edged out tried for another "post" (sometimes "losers" drop out of the group). The leader types were vying for most knowledgeable, smartest, group leader, clarifier, sergeant-at-arms. Others were not running for election at all but were finding a partner in the group to give them credibility and place. The fact that most of this happens just below the surface makes for an emotionally charged and delicate process.

Understanding Group Dynamics

Group dynamics is a complex subject that can't be developed in this book, but your grasp of how groups interact affects your ability to help the kids in your group stretch and grow. For example, how should you respond to the kid who wants to stay with his best friend for the entire trip? How can you help youths to reach out past their comfort zones and begin to unfold as social beings? How should you deal with Betty's ultimatum that she'll come on the trip if Whitney is coming, but *not* if Jessica is?

Simply understanding why your kids act this way in new groups does a lot to alleviate your confusion and frustration. You can think through each situation, combining wisdom and judgment with your personal knowledge of the youths. You can then go with a gut feeling of when it's time to go easy and when it's time to stretch your kids. Some youths need a best friend in order to ease into a group, find out what the roles are, and get a feel for what's going on. When that best friend becomes a crutch, however, you'll need to find an opportunity to help him or her integrate into the larger group.

On the road, hotel room assignments are the chief area of territorial dispute. Even the most well-adjusted kids can feel cheated if they aren't in the "right" room with the "right" people. The cumulative results of days of prayer, games, celebrations, and growth can be lost in a instant if the room assignments aren't carefully handled. I've seen it happen dozens of times. I've tried lecturing, downplaying, "meet a new friend" talks, and delivering stoic "deal with it" glares. Although no single method is guaranteed to work, one method enjoys consistent success—selecting youths to do the room assignments.

Youths Assign Themselves

Pick two kids to be responsible to go through the complete list of youths and make the room assignments. Reserve the right to nix anything that looks unhealthy. Don't pick your choosers randomly, though. Target youths who know most of the kids on the trip, who are respected by group members and therefore carry some authority among them, and are well accepted by the other youths. Give these kids the most current information on who's fighting with whom, who gets along well, and the like. Chances are they know all you know and then some.

Kids creating a rooming list invariably bump into what you knew all along—not everyone can be with a best friend. If you've chosen well, they are usually mature enough to assign themselves to room with "strangers" in the group. Because they've worked it out, they more readily accept it than if you made the arbitrary assignment. Everyone wins.

My experience suggests that girls are better suited than boys for making room assignments. Girls usually seem more sensitive to the interpersonal dynamics within a group. Still, when boys make assignments they'll invariably assign one of the more popular and mature boys with someone who hasn't yet come into his social glory. Because their peers are making the assignment, the youths all go along with it. If you did this, there would be groans and whines.

Another element of successful room assignments is housing an adult in each room. If there aren't enough adults to go around, assign an older youth to be the "adult." Pick the most loyal, mature, and responsible youth to be the room monitor, not necessarily the most popular. Assign an adult and/or mature monitor to each room prior to letting the kids begin the task of making the pairings.

Letting your kids take responsibility for room assignments, within well-defined parameters, usually results in a quiet, dignified transition from car to lodging. It's not a perfect system, but it's worked well for me—and the kids on the selection committee grow in understanding, leadership ability, and organizational skill.

$\mathcal{H}$andling Expenses on the Road

For the third time the church treasurer called me requesting the financial reports from a week-long camp I led. Although I wanted to get that report turned in, I kept putting it off. The truth is, I hadn't kept good records. I knew that when I finally sat down to piece together our expenditures, it would take an exorbitant amount of time and produce a barely passable financial report.

Cost accounting is a matter of developing a habit. Each organization has different requirements for handling money. These rules shape the habits you need to cultivate. Although no one set of rules guides all accounting procedures, the following tips may assist you in developing good tripping financial habits.

Use an Established Central Treasury

Put every penny collected for a trip into one central bank account, preferably one managed by your governing body. A third party should always confirm deposits. Keeping your own deposit records is ill-advised because it leaves you holding a major accounting and accountability risk. With all the money collected in one account, tracking (with a third party) all the money taken out of that account is simplified. If a third-party record shows a total of $2,500 collected and $2,486 expended, the financial report is easy to do. Even if expenses are slightly over budget, clear and accurate records from your central treasury activities assure your supervisors that you're tracking money responsibly.

How to Pay

While on the road, there are at least three ways to pay as you go.

☑ *Cash* is obviously the most versatile; it's good everywhere, and when it's gone you can't spend any more—so much for over-budget spending. On the other hand, cash is easily lost or stolen, easily misused, and the task of keeping receipts for every cent spent can distract your focus from the primary goals of your trip. Since carrying some cash is necessary on every trip (in many instances nothing else will do), place a small pad of paper and a pen inside your cash bag. When cash comes out, a receipt with written details goes in. At the end of the trip, turn in to the central treasury the receipts and the balance of cash left over—if there is any.

☑ *Checks* written on a youth group checking account cover spontaneous needs handily, but may have limited use on the road far from the home branch. Traveler's checks, on the other hand, work well near or far. They can be replaced if lost or stolen, and they spend easily. Even though they're called traveler's checks, they really fall into the category of cash. For each one spent keep a careful record of where and on what it was spent.

☑ *Credit cards*, generally readily accepted anywhere, provide an automatic receipt, making record keeping easier. A lost or stolen card inconveniences you, but it doesn't hurt as much as losing $570 cash. The downside of credit cards is the ease with which you can exceed your trip budget and not even know it. Between the end of your trip and the receipt of the monthly bill you can lose hours of sleep unless you kept careful records each time the card was used.

☑ *Combinations* of any of the above methods work well. Some hotels and retreat centers even bill your organization for services used.

Gaining Financial Respect

If you do a bang-up job of record keeping, detailing dates, places, and the items purchased, and are also able to track your financial activity in a clear report for the powers that be, you gain respect. Handling other people's money carries inherent risks. Be orderly and detailed and everyone will likely be satisfied.

Parables of Growth

13

I loaded up the van with a group of youths. I was to travel with them for a while. I was to lead them to the Father. I felt overcome by the burden of responsibility for this frightening task.

As we traveled I talked to the youths only of the Father. I painted the sternness of his face if the youths were to displease him. I spoke of the youths' goodness as something that would appease the Father's wrath. Driving past huge forests, I explained that the Father had the power to send all of them crashing down, struck by his shattering thunderbolts. Driving through sunshine, I was moved to speak of the greatness of the Father, who made the blazing sun. Driving by the shore, I impressed upon them that the Father's awesome power was like the tides that pummeled and shaped the shorelines.

One twilight we met the Father. The youths hid behind me. They were afraid. They would not look up into the face so loving; they remembered my pictures. They would not take the Father's hands; I was between the youths and the Father. I wondered. I had been so conscientious and intentional—so serious.

❖

I loaded up the van with a group of youths. I was to travel with them for a while. I was to lead them to the Father. It was an enormous task—so much to teach in so little time.

We hurried from place to place. One moment we pulled over to view a huge valley from a scenic overlook, while cleaning trash out of the van. The next moment we studied the confluence of two rivers as we passed high above on a new bridge offering a faster route. While the youths were questioning me about these, I hurried them on to drive through a national park. If they fell asleep, I woke them up lest they should miss something I wanted them to see. We spoke of the Father, oh yes—often and rapidly. I poured into their ears all the stories I thought they ought to know. But we were interrupted often by crashing waves on beaches, startled wildlife, sunsets giving way to stars.

One such twilight we met the Father. The youths merely glanced at him before gazing off in a dozen directions. The Father stretched out his hands. The youths were not interested enough to reach back. They dropped exhausted in their seats and fell asleep. Again I was between the youths and the Father. I wondered. I had shown them so much and taught them so many things.

❖

I loaded up the van with a group of youths. I was to travel with them for a while. I was to lead them to the Father. My heart was full of gratitude for the joyful privilege.

We traveled with measured tread, keeping a pace that matched the stamina of the youths in the group. We spoke of things the youths noticed. Once we saw children playing on the beach. We paused to listen to their laughter and to watch them stoop curiously over pearly shells the tides offered to the shore. We wondered later at how the waves played with us, dredging up their toys a few at a time for our delight. Often upon seeing a marvelous sight, we left the vehicles and walked around breathing in the wonder of it. We explored mountains and gorges looking for glinting quartz, wading in the carving streams, sometimes laughing, other times silent. Often we told stories of the Father. I told them to the youths and they retold them to me—over and over again. Sometimes we stopped to stretch in a park, finding comfort in the shade of one of the Father's trees, letting the air cool our brows, listening to the music of the breeze.

One twilight we met the Father. The eyes of the youths shone. They looked with love, trust, and eagerness into the Father's face. They put their hands into the Father's hands. I was for the moment forgotten. I was content.

❖

These three stories, adapted from an unidentified essay, illustrate that what most readies kids to experience spiritual growth on a trip is adults radiating a positive, hope-filled attitude. Growth guidelines are futile unless put in action with a joy-filled heart. Youths enjoy being with adults who want to be with them. Expect good things; look for opportunities to offer positive comments. Observe and encourage each person in the group. Remember that when you talk, kids don't. When you listen, youths slowly begin talking. Listening to your kids is a most precious gift; give it as often as you can.

The Parable of the Growing Seed

This is what the kingdom of God is like. A man scatters seed on the ground. Night and day, whether he sleeps or gets up, the seed sprouts and grows, though he does not know how. All by itself the soil produces grain—first the stalk, then the head, then the full kernel in the head. (Mark 4:26-28 NIV)

Growth—as frightening as it is energizing—occurs in everyone, but at different speeds, with different results, and in response to varying motivations. Some of us grow only when we're pushed; others grow only when called forth. Some grow in spite of great odds; others resist growth, even given the most favorable of circumstances. How do we mold and direct the spiritual growth of our kids in the face of their diversity?

Not to worry. You don't have to understand how growth happens in order for it to occur. We need only spread seeds—of faith, hope, challenge, love, promise, possibility, Christ risen, joy, laughter, passion, and so much more that God has placed within our hearts.

We don't struggle alone to stimulate growth among our kids; we're allied with the power of life itself—the creating God. We are not left to our own devices; we are given the guiding Holy Spirit. Every time a group comes together, expect growth—plan for it, work on it, pray for it. If a person doesn't grow as a result of your program, however, try not to take it personally. You can't force growth. At the same time, don't become complacent. Like John the Baptist, we messengers prepare the way by making paths straight. Absence of growth among kids may mean we've not cleared as straight a path as we'd like to believe.

Although there's no magic way to guarantee growth in kids, this chapter lists activities you can prepare which give your kids opportunities for Christian growth. Above all, show patience with young lives. Expect them to be great, but accept them if they wait.

Prayer Partners

Pairing youths to pray for each other can enhance spiritual growth. You may group kids by putting their names in a hat and then passing it around for each youth to draw a name out. People who draw their own name may return it to the hat and pull out another. (Youths who exercise this option more than once may be fishing for a particular name. Check their returned slips if you get suspicious). Another way to group prayer partners is to assign older youths with younger youths, girls with girls, boys with boys, youth group veterans with novices, and so on.

Either secret or overt prayer partners work well. Openly assigned prayer partners can eat a meal together, sit together, walk together, pray together. Secret partners, in addition to spending time in prayer, can leave small reminders that they're thinking of them. Youths can get creative when they hold a secret—a dandelion laid on the partner's pillow before bedtime, a note stuck in a carryon bag, an appropriate Bible verse creatively conveyed. At the end of the trip a whole worship service can be built around revealing prayer partners and allowing them to then go off together for a time to share feelings and thoughts.

Bosom Buddies

Close to the notion of prayer partners, this option works better for kids who are a bit nervous about praying for another on a daily basis. Instead of focusing strictly on prayer, partners watch each other to figure out a gift to give at the end of the day (or the trip or the week). These gifts shouldn't cost money. Encourage them to look for free things, or to impart a gift in words, in a song, or even physically (like an appropriate back rub). I've seen free Burger King paper crowns given to someone having a rough ride, foot massages and temple rubs, original poetry and songs. Secret partners must be sly—a back rub can be a gift, but it would have to be disguised by giving several other back rubs. Gifts can be hidden or handed to a silent third party to pass on. Anticipating revelation on the last day creates excitement.

Another kind of buddy system, which requires advance planning, is to assign each person on your trip to an adult in the church. These adults create a gift pack for their buddies, including a token gift for each day, notes of encouragement, Bible verses. The gift packs are then taken on the trip for you to parcel out at a specific time on each day of the journey.

Whether you use prayer partners or bosom buddies, keep a master list of who is responsible for whom. On occasions the gifts aren't appropriate and you need to clear up the difficulty. (Don't assume someone intentionally sabotages the experience; a participant may not understand the intent.) Also, sometimes kids receive nothing from their partners. In this case it's nice to know to whom one has to go to explore the reasons.

Daily Devotions

Early in the morning, at the beginning or ending of any significant experience, or at the end of the day, it's often natural to share a brief devotion. How it's done, how long it lasts, or what it's about is less important than your attitude toward it. Focus the content or activity of your devotion times on Christ and you'll stay within healthy parameters.

As with room assignments, devotions are most effective when handled by your kids. Inform them early that they'll be presenting a short devotion. When they ask what they should say or do, instruct them to focus on Christ—put few or no other limitations on them. Kids are wonderfully creative; the effort they put into this moment of sharing encourages them to grow up to meet the challenge.

Bible Readings/Studies

Traveling affects people differently—some sleep, some stare out the windows, some talk. Some travelers are able to read for hours, while others get physically sick just checking a map. Show sensitivity toward those who can't read while on the road. Schedule reading times into your trip while eating a picnic lunch or during rest stops. Or provide a Bible study with a theme only for those who like to study. The interested kids dig in, while those who can't or won't are not threatened. (One of the study activities might be for the students to share insights with someone who isn't doing the study.)

Loads of Bible studies available in books and magazines can be adapted to traveling. Or simply read a section of the Bible, such as the Psalms or the Gospels. The book of Acts is great road reading since it outlines the travels of another group, the apostles.

Individual Journals

Journaling can assist kids to reflect on a day or an event. While there is no limit to the styles of entries that can be made, three popular styles are logging events, keeping a diary, and reflecting on thoughts, feelings, and insights.

✔ *Logging events* with a few words about what happened and what stood out is a habit that some carry on for years. From time to time the writer rereads the journal to see how her or his life has evolved—how priorities have changed as demonstrated by events noted and focused on in the journal.

☑ *Keeping a diary* accompanies factual information with running commentary. Keeping a diary forces the writer to collect thoughts and record them in concrete ways. Diary style implies writing about oneself: "What a day! I lost my ring, broke up with my girlfriend, and lost the wrestling match! Leaving on this trip may be the best thing I've ever done. It began when ..." Consistently kept diaries trace how growth happens.

☑ *Reflective entries* represent an advanced style of journaling in which the writer reformulates the events of the day into a new context. For example: "We rode through Nebraska today. Incredible number of miles of green. While most slept, I began to realize how much we are like crops with God as the farmer. I hope I haven't slept when the Farmer was offering me insight and help on how to grow tall and true." This type of journal becomes a treasury for ideas, thoughts, and resources.

☑ *Blending many styles* is perhaps the most common experience of those who journal. When the spirit strikes, reflective entries come easy. When in a hurry, a simple recording of events will do. When a particular event holds one's attention, it's worth recording, along with the accompanying feelings and impressions.

Specialty Journals

Among many possible specialty journals, tickler or community journals have worked well for my groups.

☑ *Tickler journals* are prepared by the leader to give journaling more direction. At the top of each page, tickler phrases are written which suggest topics to be addressed: "Today, God seemed most real to me when ..." Each page has a different tickler phrase leading in a specific direction. On each new day of the trip, hand out that day's page. Here's an example of ticklers in a progression. It's an attempt to pull the writer into thinking about the struggles in befriending others and relating those experiences to Christ:

- Making new friends can be tough at times because ...
- If I could pick the characteristics of a perfect friend, they'd be ...
- Since no one is perfect, to me, the three most important traits of a friend are ...
- The biggest strengths I can offer to another as a friend would be ...
- Two things I can do on this trip to share my abilities as a friend with someone new would be ...
- Trying to be a good friend can be tough when it seems like no one cares. Christ must feel the same way when we don't pay attention to ways he tries to be a friend. I'll bet Christ feels ...
- If I were going to be a friend to others the way Jesus is a friend to me, I'd have to ...

☑ *Community journals* call for your entire group to write in one common notebook. Although it's not mandatory, encourage each person to record something each day. I keep the original community journal in a plastic Zip-Lock bag with a few pens. The paper stays relatively flat and free from dampness and goo. When someone feels inspired, the whole package goes to that person. The journal remains in plain sight throughout the trip, ready for whomever the urge might strike. Some youths draw pictures, some write zany poetry, some recall events from an unusual perspective, some record the inside slang from the trip. Upon returning home, ask someone to type or photocopy the community journal and distribute a copy to each participant as a memento of the trip. They're always a hoot to read and are kept forever.

Memory Books

This classic way to spur growth on any outing requires plenty of advance preparation. (The best ideas generally do.) At an early preparatory meeting of your group, provide material for kids to personalize their own three-ring notebook covers. They can decorate using pictures from magazines, original art, felt pens, any medium available. If possible, laminate the finished covers. With each person's trip book positively identified, prepare the contents, keeping in mind that pages will be added by the notebook owner—on the trip and even afterwards. The following sample of the possibilities barely touches what can be done with a memory book.

☑ *Hole-punched worksheets.* Each day hand out new pages that invite youths to ponder the trip theme, create reflections for devotions, and formulate thoughts to be used in a trip report to the church board.

☑ *Journal pages.* The previously discussed tickler pages can be included in a notebook like this.

☑ *Observation pages.* Handed out right after certain events, these sheets guide kids in formulating thoughts about what happened, how it affected them, how it affected others.

☑ *Bible insight pages.* Scripture readings with space to note reflections, feelings, and new insight can be used as evening or morning devotions.

☑ *Souvenir envelopes.* Include manila envelopes, three-hole punched along the side—one for each day. Inside travelers save post cards, trinkets, notes, pressed leaves, just about anything that triggers a memory.

☑ *Prayer partner reflections.* Record notes about prayer partners here—things prayed for, observations made, prayers answered. Filling this page up can also teach kids what prayer partners can do for each other.

☑ Other ideas include crossword puzzles, battleship game sheets, dot-to-dot games, tic-tac-toe sheets, logic problems, Scripture passages, poetry, reprints from magazines (by permission please)—the list is endless. Leave room for photo pages to be added later. Memory books make great viewing for parents, church finance committees, and other committees that approve things like trips, if you get my drift.

Special Meals

Why take meals in the same old way three times a day? Get creative. Institute a silent meal at which no one talks for twenty minutes. Debrief afterward. What was frustrating and why? What was of benefit and why? What was the funniest thing that happened and why?

For a crazy meal experience, feed a partner while your partner feeds you—in silence! Always take time to share insights and feelings following activities like this. What other ways are we fed by friends? When do we need people? How does God in Christ feed us daily, besides with the blessings of harvest? Try blindfolding the person being fed. Talk about trust! Was it hard to go through this? Why? Why is trust so difficult to attain and keep? Have we trusted God to ease our spiritual hunger? Our stress? Our emotional loads? If we don't trust God for these things, why? What could we do to improve our trust in God? In each other?

Meals, though common experiences, can be built into creative avenues of potential growth.

$\mathcal{L}$ast-Minute Checklist

14

Chapter

$\mathbf{A}$nyone who leads a group for an extended trip faces that gut fluttering question, "Have I got everything covered?"

When I finally think I've got everything lined up, packed, and arranged for, I close my eyes, and process away that nagging feeling of doubt by thinking through every segment of every day—each one. I head out on an imaginary journey that exactly parallels the trip I'm ready to begin. I think through leaving, seating, supper stops, paying for food, eating, bathrooms, thermoses of coffee, gas stops, check-ins, registration, room assignments, keys, unpacking.

I really enjoy this part of planning. It may take me an hour or more and leave me with a page of notes listing what is still needed. Sometimes I get through the exercise and realize that I'm ready. I must confess, however, that even after all these years, I occasionally forget some minor thing.

Two years ago on a bike trip in Vermont, we set up camp in the rain— arranging tarps and tables so we could cook and eat protected from the deluge. The cooks cooked, the repairers repaired, and the hungry, wet, cold, and sore waited in line to partake of a hot meal of spaghetti and meatballs. The meal was ready, grace was said, and then someone asked, "Mike, where's the silverware?" Fortunately, there was a small store nearby, and I covered my error in eight minutes with sturdy plastic-ware that seemed to cost about $7000 per setting.

No matter how much planning I do, thinking through each segment of each day of the trip is the best model I've found for dealing with that nagging question, "Have I got everything?"

Plan B

As I take my imaginary journey, I exercise another aspect of planning vital for peace of mind—a second plan, or a plan B. When we think through the segments of a trip, we tend to assume that every day will be sunshine and roses. That optimistic viewpoint neglects the reality of sickness, bad weather, traffic jams, breakdowns, and other serious alterations of plans. What happens then? Anticipate what problems may occur and how you might make adjustments.

Thinking through alternative options ahead of time allows you to experience the trip with much less stress. If a flat tire requires an unscheduled stop, plan-B games or activities help you bypass panic and assists other travelers to make smoother adaptations.

Follow-up

The day of departure has come. The checklists have been checked. You've done your last-minute thinking and collected and coordinated community gear. What's left? Following up!

Sometime on the day of departure, call everyone with whom you've made reservations for the journey—rental companies, campgrounds, motels. Call the first night's motel. Ask to whom you are speaking; introduce yourself as well. Ask how the weather is. Check location and directions—get landmarks visible in the dark if you'll be coming in at night. Let them know you're ready to leave, that you expect to arrive at such a time, and you hope to have the agreed upon number of rooms ready for your group. Double check the prices.

Finish by using the name of the person you're speaking to and say, "I'll see you in a few hours." Simple, short, direct, and very effective for making sure things turn out as planned. Make yourself and your group memorable and expected. Let them know that it's just a few hours until you have a chance to meet. Put them on notice. Most desk people are ready, but if you've ever met one who didn't have a clue as to who you were or what you wanted, you'll understand the wisdom of this advice.

Confirm reservations the day you depart, especially if you made your reservations months in advance. Just because a deposit was sent in doesn't mean that all will be ready for you. In all my years of travel, this single step has proved its worth. I can't begin to tell you how many times things like rooms, costs, and such had to be corrected, adjusted, or clarified when everything was supposed to be all set. Paperwork can get set aside, lost, and otherwise goofed up. Help the organizations look good and help yourself at the same time. Give them some warning—time to cover their errors if they need it.

One time I reserved six hotel rooms in upstate New York for kids on a bike trip. The night before we left, I called to let them know we would be there the next evening. We had no rooms. It seemed that a local woman was having a big wedding, and all the rooms were required for the guests attending. Our whole group got bumped, and they never bothered to call and let me know. I could imagine getting there, tired, late, and hungry, only to have them look at me like I was some good ol' Georgia boy who was powerful lost. It took the better part of an hour and some major changes in our itinerary to correct that mess. Still, I was pleased to do it from the comfort of my office rather than on the fly with eighteen road-weary sojourners looking at me like I was an administrative disaster.

Following up prevents fouling up!

Part Three

GO!

At last! After all the planning the group takes to the road.

The magic of traveling together provides unique and wonderful opportunities for growth and friendship. Traveling together also challenges the travelers to consider new perspectives and to defer to each other—at bathroom stops, while sharing cramped space, when feeling tired and cranky. Some kids feel cold when others are too hot. Some like loud music, while others get a headache from the bass. Some enjoy frank discussions and jokes; others are offended. The way you handle issues like these—and more—can make the difference between a dream trip and a trip that becomes a nightmare.

$\mathcal{P}$lanning for Stops

Vehicle #3 radios you—a kid has to use the bathroom. You begin to look for a stop with a bathroom. Shortly you pull into a small gas station. The youth anxiously trotting through its front door starts a chain reaction—nearly everyone else suddenly decides they also need to go. Meanwhile a few remaining in the vans decide they need a soda. A new line forms at the cash register that rivals the bathroom line. And of course those exiting the bathrooms decide to get a snack as well. What should have been a two-minute break turns into a thirty-minute dawdle. No wonder trippers are so often behind schedule.

Twenty years and many thousand miles of tripping later, the all-time winners for most frequent stops are food, gas, and bathrooms. In an ideal world these three would be contained in one road stop. Imagine—after three hours on the road the caravan pulls off to gas up. You announce: "Restrooms are in the station, and we'll pick up lunch at the burger place across the parking lot. See you all in twenty minutes."

Unfortunately, the big three happen in random order, without logical sequence, and seldom at the same time. A seasoned tripper can, however, maximize the effectiveness of stops, while minimizing the time used, by planning wisely and thinking ahead.

A One, a Two . . .

Before a group leaves any place, from the very first stop to the very last, they must adhere to the cardinal group travel rule for stopping safety: the head count. There are many ways to make sure no one gets left behind. Here are three common yet effective ones.

☑ *Roll call.* As you read each person's name from a roster, that person responds with, "Here." The group rolls ahead only when the list checks out. Roll call automatically identifies missing members. It's not as effective with more than one vehicle, however—most kids want to jump around among the vehicles, which frustrates the caller.

☑ *Assigning numbers.* Also most effective with one vehicle, each traveler receives a number for the entire event. Prior to each departure, the youths count off in order from number one until all are accounted for. Match missing numbers to the numbered names on your list to identify the person to hunt for.

A major drawback to both roll calls and numbers is that even in the most well-behaved groups, a prankster may answer for a missing person—just to be funny, or because he or she thinks the other person's on board already. The larger the group, the more nagging the possibility.

☑ *Head count.* Effective in just about any setting, head counting bypasses uncertainties by verifying that a trip that begins with seventeen people, departs every stop with exactly seventeen heads counted. Give the head counting task to one person alone, rather than letting three or four count and then add up subtotals. Don't let individual drivers do their own counting, either. Kids move from vehicle to vehicle and counts can change.

If someone is late returning to the vehicle, *never* leave her or him behind—even if it means your group misses an important event or reservation.

In Toronto, Canada, my group of fifteen was to gather at our hotel to catch our train home. Four kids were not at the rendezvous in time for our departure. After changing our tickets to a later train, I called the church to warn parents we were behind schedule. When the absent youths arrived, pale, frightened, and out of breath, they explained they'd gotten turned around at a large mall and couldn't find their way back to the hotel. Once we healed fears and talked about what could have been done differently, we made plans to do something fun. After all, everyone was okay—and now we had extra time.

The Art of the Fast Food Stop

Choose your food stop with your group size in mind. Ten or twelve can be served by any fast food restaurant in a matter of minutes. Thirty or forty famished travelers, however, can overwhelm a fast food restaurant. Given the corresponding long, slow counter lines, the first half of the group will be finished eating and bored before the second half even receives its order.

A restaurant strip is better equipped to serve larger groups, however, for both speed and food preferences. A strip, that battlefield of a street where all the national chains fight it out head to head, offers kids everything from breakfast tacos to yogurt to chicken on a stick—all within a safe walk from the parking space. Give the youths thirty minutes, spread adults throughout, and enjoy. The shopping mall food court also easily handles large crowds. In thirty minutes kids can cover all the bases—eat, go to the bathroom, stretch, and buy new batteries.

For a moderate size group, fast food stops are not the only option. With plenty of time and a desire to work a bit, supermarket buying for a rest stop picnic provides a fresh change of pace. Eating in the vehicle works, but poorly. Since stops are a necessary part of traveling, allow time to eat out. It pays dividends later in the form of peaceful en route naps for your travelers and cleaner vehicles at the day's end.

Gas Stop Magic

Seek out a facility equal to the task of handling your size group. Trailers in tow, for instance, need wider lots to negotiate a turnaround, and low overhangs may be disastrous. One or two vehicles can get gas anywhere. Five vans and a school bus require large stations. I've seen groups leave half their caravan in the street because their group instantly filled all pump lanes. For the quickest gas stop, you need a free pump for each vehicle. The slowest way is to fill all the tanks from one pump and pay one big tab when you finish. Due to poor planning, I once stood for forty-five minutes filling all the tanks from one pump.

Prior to pulling into a gas station, let the passengers know if a stop is a pure gas stop—meaning no food or drink purchases, and no bathroom breaks allowed. If youths anticipate a stop, their bladders and stomachs pick up the cue and beg for relief. Once those internal triggers are tripped, nothing can reverse the need. With advance warning, riders seem to be able to quell the urge before it picks up steam. Though this has no basis in medical fact, twenty years on the road have proven the truth of it to me.

Emergency requests, of course, take priority over most restrictions. Even then keep a tight rein. One or two riders using the bathroom or one or two carsick riders buying a soda can prompt a mass migration. Also, forbid buying and drinking sixty-four ounce soft drink specials. In less than thirty-five minutes that amount of liquid needs to be recycled at yet another emergency bathroom stop. Generally youths are receptive to the idea of hurrying or holding off if it means they'll get to the destination quicker.

Bathroom Stops

When a kid says, "I've *got* to go!" take her or him seriously. Kids often wait until the last possible moment in an attempt to not bother the group. When someone actually announces the issue to everyone, it's serious.

The very best bathroom stops are public highway rest areas, which offer plenty of space for any number of vehicles to park and plenty of rooms to rest in. Equally important, there are no stores enticing youths to consume things that will dictate yet another premature bathroom stop. Grassy areas are great for passing footballs or tossing discs, shade cools travelers as they lie down, and litter barrels are plentiful.

As you approach a rest area, ask yourself if it's been a few hours since you last stopped. If the answer is yes, pull off. I guarantee everyone will appreciate it. If after several hours of uninterrupted driving no rest area is imminent, stop at a gas station or fast food restaurant. Park where gas pump lines won't be blocked and you won't interfere with customers.

*C*aravan Rules and Convoy Safety

16

Chapter

W hy are you driving so fast up front?"

"Whaddaya mean? I only went over sixty one time to pass a tractor."

"Then why have I been driving seventy-five since I left the church parking lot?"

"It must be your speedometer, 'cause I've been real careful."

Some mysteries in the universe defy explanation. The following is one of those unexplained riddles: While a lead vehicle in a caravan drives a constant fifty-five miles per hour, the last vehicle in that caravan has to travel seventy-five miles per hour to keep up. The discrepancy is the number-one gas stop discussion among caravan drivers. A caravan is two or more vehicles following one another. Large caravans can consist of a dozen vehicles or more. What works for two vehicles works for many—though it requires more concentration.

Good Driver Profile

Few groups have the luxury of choosing the most qualified drivers among many applicants. Some youth workers feel fortunate to find even one minimally quali-fied adult willing to make a short trip. Nonetheless, it's imperative to identify safe, mature drivers that enjoy traveling with youths. If this kind of driver is also a committed Christian whose behavior demonstrates true faith and who loves God's children, it's a bonus. Should you have to choose either a marginal church person who loves kids, drives safely, and is a helpful team member, or a com-mitted Christian who hasn't got a gift of living in an enclosed space with youths for hours on end, has difficulty communicating, and whose driving skills are in question, take the first one. The kids can be powerful witnesses to your drivers. I've seen many adults grow in their Christian faith and church commitment as a result of a well-planned trip.

A driver worth selecting is characterized by the following:

☑ *Maturity behind the wheel.* Mothers and fathers have entrusted to your chosen driver their most beloved possessions, their children. Second chances are not guaranteed in the event of a wreck. Your drivers must drive safely. The immature volunteer driver can be tempted to impress riders with high-risk behavior. Most youths love a thrill, and aggressive driving elicits oh's and ah's. The best drivers don't give in to this subtle lure to show off behind the wheel.

Because impressionable youths are learning from their example, those behind the wheel must also drive wisely. Racing for position, leapfrogging on the freeway, weaving about, trying to pass items from vehicle to vehicle—these "games" leave a dangerous imprint. Youths may feel it's okay for them to drive this way.

☑ *Special training.* Ideally, require all of your drivers to take a defensive driving course, often available from a local vocational education program. Such a course updates drivers on changes in DMV code and reacquaints them with methods of safe driving. At the very least, each prospective driver must provide you with current proof of insurance and driver's license number. A driver who can't provide this information doesn't drive. Requiring a training course among your other regulations gives you an out with a volunteer driver you feel is unqualified. Some adults simply are not ready to drive for a group. By insisting on certain requirements, you protect your right of final choice over drivers.

☑ *Passenger awareness.* Every driver ought to share one vital experience with their riders—riding in the back of the vehicle for a whole day. Many drivers innocently assume everyone on board is as comfortable as they are—adequate ventilation, appropriate radio volume, and decent leg room. In truth, even the hardiest youths get restless, cramped, and bored in the back. Drivers who know these symptoms are better prepared to help riders cope. I've never met the driver that didn't grow from this experience.

Additionally, good drivers sense how to help the youths interact while traveling. Chatting with riders, suggesting games, or starting a songfest can help kids feel more comfortable. Occasionally, long rides bring on goofy behavior—angry, hostile, zany, just about anything imaginable. Good drivers see beyond the obvious to understand what's going on.

If your drivers don't come equipped with good communicative and interactive skills, consider offering a preparatory workshop. Get youths and drivers together to role play the upcoming trip on chairs set up to resemble the interior of a vehicle. The youths play the drivers and the drivers play the youths. Mix and match groupings to act out the participants' perceptions of helpful and not-so-helpful behaviors. After the laughter and the denials have subsided, discuss helpful responses to travel experiences that reflect Christian expectations.

☑ *Minimum age.* Strive to enlist drivers twenty-five and older. Most insurance companies require drivers of groups to be at least twenty-one. Check it out with the company that insures the vehicles you'll use. Also, check to see if your organization's policy dictates a minimum age for drivers.

One final note on age: *Never* at any time let one of the kids take the wheel.

☑ *Let the kids be kids.* In twenty years of road tripping, I've noticed that drivers who experience difficulties share a common trait—they had trouble with kids behaving like, well—kids! Teens like music, noise, laughter, and junk food. Youths are spontaneous and unpredictable—quiet and serene one minute, and off the van's walls the next. Traveling is integral to the youth trip experience, and grumpy drivers who don't want the radio on and expect everyone to sit quietly work against your goals.

The best drivers can insulate themselves from the chaos going on in the back, yet are easily roused from their concentration upon hearing their name called. They warmly respond when the kids need a bit of adult direction to keep safe.

Getting Out Of Town Together

Your caravan, poised to exit the church parking lot, waits for the lead vehicle to enter the traffic pattern. By the time vehicle #2 pulls into the congestion, it's separated from the lead by three cars. The last vehicle to venture forth is one right turn and a stop light away from the lead. In an instant all six vehicles are beyond visual range, and the driver who thought they'd chosen the other route out of town pulls into the wrong turn lane. You haven't even left the city and half the drivers have tension headaches.

Getting out of town can go smoothly if you make a prior arrangement to meet together at a designated spot at the edge of town. With the first rendezvous set where traffic and stop lights won't work against you, you can really begin your trip—and leave the Excedrin in the glove compartment for later.

The plan even works in a strange city. Designate on the area's maps in each car a place to rendezvous near a highway exit or at a rest area. It only takes a minute, and it's worth every second of that in terms of comfort and peace of mind. If one of your drivers gets disoriented and cannot find the prearranged stop, the driver should return to the starting point. Discourage uninformed driving around to look for the others. If a car does not show up at the rendezvous point after a certain amount of time, send a driver back to retrieve the stray vehicle.

Vehicle Pacing

The speed of travel is decided by law—drivers must follow posted speed limits. If you've done much driving, however, you know some situations require modifications. Any vehicle traveling fifty-five miles per hour at rush hour on Atlanta's I-285, for instance, will probably cause an accident. The minimum rush hour speed edges closer to sixty-five. For that reason I plan travel times to avoid any major city during rush hour, morning or night. Take an extra long stop for food, start earlier, start later, look at alternative routes—do anything that keeps you off busy roads during rush hours. Even during normal traffic, however, a four-car caravan traveling at the posted speed limit is among the slower vehicles on the road. That's okay.

Let me share a nightmare that keeps me traveling at posted speeds. My vanload of six kids and I are running a tad late for our destination. Rather than stop to make a phone call, I figure I can pick up a few minutes by pushing my speed. I am traveling fully ten miles over the speed limit when there's an explosive accident. Two kids on the back bench are killed. In my nightmare I next see myself trying to defend the situation: I was careful. I was awake. I was in control. Sure, I was speeding, but only by ten miles over the limit! After that last admission, there are no more questions. The cold bare fact is that I intentionally did wrong. My error in judgment cost the lives of two teens entrusted to my care. I wake up in a cold sweat.

Travel the speed limit at all times. If the flow of traffic pressures you to speed, get off the road or out of the way—but don't give in. In the event of an accident, you'll be glad you followed the laws.

Speed of travel is only one part of the equation of vehicle pacing. The second part is the physical distance between vehicles in a caravan. Just as there's never a good reason for speeding, there's never a good reason to bunch up. Crowding invites danger. Resist the tendency to narrow the gap between vehicles in the caravan in order to discourage other drivers from cutting into the caravan. Each vehicle in your caravan needs to leave several car lengths between themselves. Spread out a bit. Driving in a bunch denies other vehicles the opportunity to lawfully pass. With proper spacing others can pass your caravan in stages. Bunching, on the other hand, entices drivers to pass in dangerous ways. Leave your headlights on for safety, identifying each vehicle as part of a team. (This also allows the lead vehicles to easily check on the others.) If one driver stays too close to another vehicle, clarify the procedure at the next stop.

You're Late, Now What?

It's 6:00 p.m. and you told parents you'd be home by seven—yet you're still two hours from home. You envision twelve vehicles occupied by twelve glaring parents as you pull in late ... again!

The art of moving many persons in an orderly fashion seems colored in chaos. But it doesn't have to be that way. Timeliness necessitates only two things—leaving a place on time and arriving at a destination on time.

☑ *Leaving on time* is a strategy of communication and training. Some leaders schedule the group meeting time thirty minutes before they plan to leave the parking lot. After the first few times, though, the youths catch on. They translate a 6:00 deadline to mean 6:30 and dribble in closer to 7:00. For the sake of clear communication, break down departure into timed stages. Write up a schedule like the following:

- 5:30—Load luggage until 6:15.
- 6:15—Parents and youths gather for last minute instructions and prayer.
- 6:25—Get into vehicles to pull out of parking lot at precisely 6:30.

Those who pull in at 6:32 weren't a mere two minutes late. They were an hour and two minutes late, which isn't something you must tolerate.

☑ *Arriving on time* is the other half of timeliness. Getting youths to places late is a common experience. Few things about group trips happen as quickly as we hope, primarily because schedules are erroneously based on normal travel experiences. Traveling with groups is not normal—everything with groups takes longer.

The best way to handle tardiness is to stop and notify those at the destination by phone. Though it's inconvenient and makes arrival later than ever, the first step to dealing with being late is to admit it—like with any addiction. A call reduces anxiety for all concerned and allows people time to adjust. Parents especially are always relieved to know the status of a delayed caravan.

To be certain you're not pulling off the road to make phone calls at every turn, use the E.T.A.—Estimated Time of Arrival. The key word is *estimated*. Give out a helpful estimation of arrival—specific enough to allow people to make plans; vague enough to allow yourself some latitude. Instead of saying you'll be there about seven, say you hope to be in sometime between seven and eight. Tell parents not to come to pick up their children up until their child calls. The few minutes it takes parents to drive to the pick up point can be used for your kids to clean out the vehicles.

If you're late beyond even your estimated arrival time, phoning home is a must. An efficient way to prepare for possible lateness—or any other trip changes or troubles—is to designate a parent or other adult before you leave to be the contact person for this trip. Print the contact's name, address, and phone number on index cards to be handed out to parents as they drop their youths prior to leaving. Using the phone you regularly update the designated adult. Now, any other parents needing travel updates can call the contact person for the latest. Provide your contact with a list of the phone numbers of all persons on the trip. In emergencies, the contact person not only receives calls from others but can place them as well.

Whoops, You've Lost the Group

Imagine heading out of New Orleans with a three-car caravan into a breath-taking sunrise. Within minutes you're no longer enjoying the view, however, because your caravan has been split up by heavy traffic and a major fork in the road lies just ahead. While the kids in the lead van are waving and shouting to get the attention of the other drivers, the last van is cut off before it can get in the correct lane. As smooth as you please, it's sucked into a maze of overpasses, underpasses, forks, and loops. What do you do? I suggest the "pay phone check in."

It works like this. Three parties are involved—the caravan, the lost party(ies), and a third person who has agreed to stay near his or her phone (at work or at home). Should a caravan get split up, both parties stop to call the third party, who takes phone numbers from both callers. Now the split parties are able to contact each other through the pay phones to arrange a meeting spot. Both parties must pull off to make their phone calls as soon as possible, as well as watch for names of cross streets or off ramps that identify their locations—"I'm heading north on Highway 25, six miles off of Route 85. I'm at a Joe's restaurant, and the phone number is such and so." If by chance the emergency check-in person doesn't answer the phone, wait at your pay phone until you can reach him.

Another method is to agree that any lost vehicle turn around and make its way back to the correct route. The lead vehicle meanwhile pulls off and remains visible until both are reunited. Though this can work, being out of contact with each other creates a lot of anxiety. It's best to plan a way to talk to each other as soon as possible.

Changing Drivers and Resting Engines

Any vehicle is only as good as the care it receives. Driving fast and hard takes a toll on the engine. Think about a vehicle as a finite entity; treat it kindly as you would its passengers. Does it need oil? Water? Rest? Is the engine making new noises, indicating it needs attention? While no one likes to add time to a trip, dealing with potential problems when it's convenient is preferable to ignoring warnings until you're stuck in the middle of nowhere.

I've also learned that drivers need rest and attention, too. If possible, change drivers every 200 miles or four hours. Keep an alert person behind the wheel.

Maps For Everyone

There was a day when I believed that if the lead driver knew where he or she was going, that was enough. The other cars could simply follow. No longer.

On one fateful trip two work teams headed out on a week-long mission project to towns twenty-five miles apart. Before separating, the drivers agreed to reconnoiter at a specific crossroads at the end of the week. They picked a road (without the benefit of a map) that they thought intersected a common county road about halfway between the two work sites. At the end of the week group A waited at the appointed time and place. After nearly two hours, deciding that group B wasn't going to show, group A headed on to that night's destination alone.

Fortunately, clear directions to that night's lodgings had been given. Group A arrived about a half an hour before group B. Comparing notes, the drivers discovered that group B had also waited two hours, but at a different intersection of identical description. The chosen road intersected at several different places along the common county road. A cup of coffee and a few chuckles brought this episode to a close. But it could have been a disaster. Fully half of the group was lost, and no one had any idea of how or where to begin finding one another.

Every driver needs to know the basics about where the trip is going from start to finish.

- Provide for each driver a map of all the territory you'll be covering.
- Highlight on each driver's map the primary route the group will take.
- List on each driver's map the phone numbers of each place you're headed, along with all relevant emergency numbers.
- At a meeting of drivers prior to your trip, hand out the maps to review and discuss the routes and destinations.

You're then ready to head out!

*V*an Games

T he CB radio crackled to life in the lead van: "We need a bathroom stop back here." The announcement failed to animate the sluggish kids, even though they had traveled almost three hours without a stop. The driver pondered how to rouse them to find their shoes and money. Turning down the music, he announced that they had five minutes to prepare for a fifteen-minute bathroom and gas break.

Not satisfied that the stretching and yawning travelers could sufficiently energize themselves for a quick stop, the driver yelled out, "Left hand on right window." Lurching and bumping each other, the travelers complied. He followed his first command with "Right foot on left window." Grunts and thuds testified to more energetic attempts. Then, "Left foot on ceiling," "Left hand on floor," "Right hand on left window," followed in quick succession. The lethargic youths of a few minutes ago were transformed into a teeming mass of laughter and intertwined legs and arms straining for proper location.

When they spilled out onto the parking area at the stop, their raucous hilarity attracted stares. This was the genesis of Van Twister.

Group travel occasionally benefits from an activity that works inside your van. Youth trippers from all over the country use and recommend the following games and activities. Enjoy and use them as a springboard to create new ones.

Crossword Puzzles

Not many youths consider themselves smart enough to do crosswords. Yet when an adult starts asking for words of so many letters fitting different clues, nearly everyone wants to guess. Before long, an entire vehicle can be wrapped up in doing a crossword puzzle. With a pencil and a few individuals that enjoy a challenge, this can be a great group builder. With CB units, it even works between vehicles.

CB Lyric Wars

This popular game requiring CB units can painlessly while away a few hours. One van's group (team A) picks a word to tell to the group in a second van (team B). Team B confers together for thirty seconds or less to identify at least 8 words of a popular song containing the chosen word. The team must then successfully sing the lyric into the CB unit. Then it's team A's turn. They have thirty seconds in which to choose a different song whose lyrics contain the same word and sing at least eight words. The teams continue back and forth until one group cannot (within thirty seconds) think of any more songs containing that word. The team that last sang receives points for doing so. Continue the game with team B selecting a new word.

Rather than choosing a word, a team may select a category or theme. The category "songs about cars," for instance, might inspire the Beach Boys' "Fun, fun, fun, till her daddy takes the T-bird away." Teams then take turns singing lines from songs about any aspect of cars. When one team runs out of car songs, points are awarded to the other team and a new category is chosen. Everybody gets in on this game and everyone can help win. Please note, the lyrics must be sung.

CB Story Lines

Though this CB game starts slow, once a few good yarn spinners get it going everyone usually jumps in. Begin by asking a question like, "How did that town (street, lake, whatever) get its name?" From that, one team begins a story, and the next team adds a paragraph or a complete thought to it. The starting team then adds more to the story, and so it goes until everyone agrees the story is done. All trippers can contribute to the creative legend.

Objects

In this two-person game, one chooses the left side of the road and the other chooses the right side. Players must identify an object that begins with every letter in the alphabet in order. "I see an airplane for A," "I see a barn for B," and so on. The only rule is that once an object has been used, it can't be used again by either person. If "car" is used for the letter C, for example, then nothing on a car can be used for the rest of the game. Likewise, naming "automobile" eliminates the chance to use "car." The game moves quickly and needs little concentration.

Signs

Much like in Objects, the two players in this game choose opposite sides of the road. The goal is to find each letter of the alphabet on a sign along the way. Letters have to be seen in order, and only one letter may be chosen from each sign.

Categories

This game works just like Lyric Wars, except teams take turns naming items in categories instead of singing songs lyrics. If team one chooses "movie stars," then each team has up to thirty seconds to name a movie star until one team comes up dry. Try categories like Bible Characters, Musicals, and others.

"Going Out West" (or East, or North, or South)

Start this old classic by saying, "I'm going out west, and I'm taking my guitar." The next player says the same line and adds an item: "I'm going out west, and I'm taking my guitar and my cat." Before players can say what they are taking, they must recite in order what everyone else is taking. After going around the circle three or four times, memories get fuzzy and the items more outrageous.

Hand-Holding Murderer

Prepare for this game by putting one slip of paper per player in a hat or a shoe. Mark one slip of paper with an X. Everyone draws a paper, and the person who draws the X becomes the secret murderer.

The group manages a rough circle with everyone holding hands, and the murderer begins the grisly task of killing off people in the circle one by one. To kill someone the murderer sends out a series of hand squeezes. Let's say Bob is the killer. Terry, his intended target, is three persons to Bob's left. Between Bob and Terry are Jenny and Laura, in that order. Bob squeezes Jenny's hand three times. Jenny then squeezes Laura's hand one time less than the number she herself received—two times. Laura then squeezes Terry's hand one less squeeze— one time. Terry cannot subtract any squeezes, which means he's been killed.

Players who are killed announce they are dead. They remain in the circle, passing squeezes without subtracting any, but they cannot guess who the killer might be. Squeezes can go in either direction, but they can't be reversed in the middle. A player whose left hand is squeezed passes the appropriate number of squeezes with his right hand to the next player's left hand.

After each murder, players who are not dead may attempt to guess the identity of the murderer. In the above example, Jenny may guess, but she doesn't know if Bob received four squeezes from the other hand he was holding and passed the three to her or if Bob was the originator. When someone guesses the killer's identity, players return their papers to the hat and pass it again to begin another round.

A popular variation is to kill people by winking at them. Players receiving a wink announce they are dead and are unable to guess until the next round. The killer must wink when only one person is looking at her. Any "nondead" players who observe a wink of death intended for another player are free to guess who the killer is.

Twenty Questions
In this old standby that still works to pass time and tax imaginations, players guess what a person is thinking of in twenty questions or less. The only clue the person who is "It" gives at the beginning is whether the object is animal, vegetable, or mineral. People don't fit in any of those categories.

Start simple and work up to tricky. Something simple easily fits into one of the three above categories—an emerald, for instance, which is a mineral. An object like a book is trickier—it's printed on paper, which is made from wood, and therefore qualifies for the vegetable category.

Battleship

Photocopy sheets like the one on page 140. Players draw in their battleships, covering the specified number of spaces for each boat type. Players take turns "firing" three consecutive salvos anywhere on their opponents' grids by calling out coordinates (for instance, A,3; A,4; A,5). When attacked, players first record the three shots on their own large grid and then announce any hits. Players don't indicate which shots hit and which ones missed. A player must say when a boat has been sunk, however. Attackers record salvos fired on the small grid. Players who sink all their opponents' ships win.

Magnetic Games

A host of magnetic board and pegboard games are available these days at a very reasonable price—Travel Cribbage, Yahtzee, Parcheesi, checkers, chess, and so much more. These can be well worth the moderate expense.

Tongue Twisters

Kids enjoy trying to master tongue twisters. Here are but a few of thousands out in the world. Good luck. Good Luck. Lood Gluck.

- Toy boat
- Peter Piper picked a peck of pickled peppers
- Six, slippery, slimy snakes sleep soundly
- She sells sea shells by the seashore
- Bobby polished black boots blacker
- Rubber baby buggy bumpers

As the miles roll away, these and other games can keep trippers occupied. You can even create tests, like naming all the capitals of all the states or all the teams in the National Basketball Association. Even word games like Sniglets can be fun. Sniglets are new words to describe common occurrences. What's a word for when the lady in the grocery check-out line doesn't even begin to get her checkbook out of her purse until after the total is rung up and announced? I don't know what it is, but I've been calling these folks names for years.

Games work best when kids are in the mood. Suggest a game and see what the response is. If it gets a thumbs down at the moment, don't force it. Try it again later. Wait a few minutes, then suggest another game.

Battleship!

	A	B	C	D	E	F	G	H	I	J
1										
2										
3										
4										
5										
6										
7										
8										
9										
10										

Place your ships and record your opponent's bombing strategy here.

- Players draw in their ships in consecutive squares on their large grids. Boats may be vertical or horizontal but never diagonal. Two boats may never share a square.
- As player A calls out three consecutive bombing coordinates, he records his attack on his small grid.
- Once the player under attack records on her large grid the results of the attack, she must report how many hits were made, if any. She does not tell which squares were a hit or on which ship the hit was made.
- Player B then calls out three bombing coordinates on her opponent in the same manner.
- When a ship is fully sunk, the players must identify which boat it was.
- First player to finish sinking all the opponent's navy wins the game.

Each player draws in:

A four-square aircraft carrier

A three-square cruiser

A three-square battleship

A three-square destroyer

A two-square patrol boat

Record your bombing missions here.

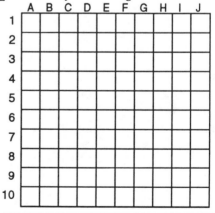

Music Management

At long last, sixteen kids and four adults piled into a yellow school bus, starting a three-day trip to Wyoming for a backpacking experience. The old bus was equipped with seats, some working windows, and little else—no music, no air conditioning, no reclining seats. The leader, convinced that any form of music not coming from the lips of the riders was divisive and unnecessary, banned radio or cassette players. Other adult staff, however, felt that a few tunes would ease the long, hot, boring hours aboard the antique bus. "Folks can sing along, talk, or ignore it," they reasoned. "No. Radios and tapes block the natural development of communication," the leader responded. He viewed music as an easy escape, a way to avoid developing relationships.

The problem is, of course, that both sides are correct. Music, even as background, can be just enough of a distraction to dampen dialogue. Especially when someone yells, "Turn up the radio; that's my favorite song!" Yet we've also gone miles without music and still no conversation. The silence can be as maddening as inane noise. In fairness, it's common for a group to struggle only briefly with silence, then magically move into enthusiastic conversation. However, I've also seen awkward silence broken by conversation focused on a popular song playing through the speakers. In those cases a little music was the common denominator to get people talking (or at least humming along).

The Walkman adds another twist—without bothering anyone else, or being bothered by anyone else, kids can drop out of the group altogether, escaping into the world of their favorite music. I'm never sure if they're sleeping or just resting their eyes while they tune in the music and tune out the rest of the group.

To Play or Not to Play?

So how do youth workers manage music on a trip? Those I talked to all allow music on trips. It's part of being a youth. The real struggle isn't to play or not to play, but *what* to play.

One Virginia youth worker bases his rule of thumb for music choice on Jesus' answer to a question about unclean hands. He taught that it's not what goes into people that defiles them, but what comes out of their hearts and minds. This youth worker suggests that if the music evokes images no one would be embarrassed for others to see, don't worry about it. On the other hand, if the song describes behavior you don't want to cultivate, why play it?

Several youth leaders limit the music choices to groups recording on a Christian music label. Others, wanting to encourage singing along, bump any bands screeching unintelligible lyrics in favor of bands performing singable and well-known tunes. The best recommendation among the majority of road veterans is to allow a blend of what's good for everyone, youths and adults alike.

On-the-road experience teaches you to sense the rhythms of traveling. The time of day, the number of trip days ahead, what activity the group is doing—these all influence the rhythm. Leaving the parking lot at the beginning of a journey is usually an energizing time. If your group leaves on a Friday evening after a full day of school, expect the evening mellows to set in four hours after dusk. As travel days unfold, mornings are gentle, afternoons are spacey, evenings are varied. Coming home is sleepy time, leaving home is zombie time. Meals are rowdy, hot afternoons lazy. Different rhythms call for varying styles of music—and sometimes no music.

Nighttime oldies sing-a-longs inspire participation. Hot afternoons can be perfect for private listening and sleeping. Sudden lulls can be used for impromptu lip syncing, using Tootsie Roll Pops for microphones. Spice mornings with easy listening and jazz. The key is variety.

The Youth Music Manager
Assigning kids to handle the selection of group music raises in them a flurry of questions—

- What kind of music should we listen to?
- Whose tastes do we appeal to?
- Should we limit music to only those bands and singers that profess to live Christian lives?
- Should we allow all music, except what's totally vile and disgusting to even the most jaded of listeners?
- What if one person loves classical synthesizer music, while another person despises it?

Kids prompted to ask these questions learn greater sensitivity to others' tastes, a fuller awareness of lyric content, and creative use of music for games, sing-a-longs, and entertainment. Choose your youth music managers early enough to give them time to think through their choices of music. It's one of the toughest jobs a youth can be given; in fact, many refuse it. There's nothing like music to bring out the whiners in a group—"Who picked this garbage?" "Man, do we have to listen to this?" "Isn't there anything else to listen to besides this junk?" Let it slip out that anyone who complains too loudly is an automatic choice for music manager for the next trip.

Mixed Tape Competitions

Rolling down the freeway in holiday traffic, I'm trying to stay out of the way of big rigs doing seventy-five. While my eyes dart from side mirror to rearview, I hear my name from the back of the van: "Mike, will you put this tape in?"

When traffic lets up for a moment, I pop the tape in the deck. The same voice yells out, "Fast forward it to the third song." I oblige. I press play at about where I think the third song might be, and the anonymous voice yells out, "Not that side. Flip it over and go back." Finally finding the song, I let it play. When it's over, a new voice presses in from the back of the van: "Mike, can you play this tape? Fifth song on side B."

I call this the Jukebox Driver Game. It's one of my pet peeves.

One trip a young lady unintentionally beat this trap. She handed me a tape, and I instinctively asked, "Which side?" "It doesn't matter," she said. "It's a mixed tape I made up myself." Popping it into the deck treated the entire group to a mix of songs many of us loved but hadn't heard in months, even years. Each song was by a different artist, and the blend was a blessing and a relief.

Before our next trip, which was a cruise to the Bahamas, I issued a challenge. Contestants must tape a mix of music having island/beach themes. The youth who prepared a tape with the widest appeal among our own group, as judged by frequency of requests to play it, would win a gift certificate to the local record store. Kids rifled their collections to cull out the perfect songs with fantastic results. Tape after tape played to approval and applause. Not once did anyone ask to change a tape or whine about a song or band. Some of the tapes were great; a few were fantastic.

Gift incentives have long since passed, but each trip is graced by a bevy of mixed tapes that reflect our destination—all prepared in advance, and all unique and enjoyable. As a side benefit, when the tapes are pulled out years later, we instantly recall old trips, replete with memories and stories.

Method to Your Music

If music is truly as important to youths as we are led to believe, we need to take it seriously. Youths know a great deal about their music, and they take pride in it. Allowing them to be responsible and creative and thrusting them into a process that challenges them to be more sensitive and aware seems to be a perfect way to manage the music—not just for one trip, but for a lifetime.

*H*otel and Motel Management

19

Chapter

Taking a group of kids to a motel almost guarantees you'll get to know the security guard and the night desk clerk who sends him. Hotels can bring out the Mr. Hyde in teen personalities. Whether you must interrupt kids jumping on beds or between balconies, or put a damper on kids blasting the TV, how can you manage a group of adrenaline-crazed youths without coming off as an ogre?

The following suggestions blend tips from many youth leaders. While I've observed that if kids have a mind to pull something nothing stops them, I still believe precautions can help turn chaos into control in hotels.

An Adult in Every Room

If possible, put an adult in every room. It only makes sense when one trip objective is to assist adults to spend time listening to, talking and playing with, and teaching youths. Grouping kids with adults according to hotel room assignments naturally breaks large groups into manageable discussion clusters. For another thing, room checks are never necessary. Interspersed with young roommates, responsible adults oversee their charges easily. You merely announce a curfew and let overseers put it to work. You'll discover another benefit at check-out—each room has a person to wake up the kids, hurry them through the shower, recheck under beds during packing, and get kids to the vehicles with gear in hand.

In groups where too few adults accompany travelers, tap one of the youths to assume adult responsibility for a room. I've found that the best kids to press into service are the quiet, shy ones—provided their roommates are compliant and mature. Some leaders are tempted to award the wrong youths with this assignment. Instead of getting an acting adult, they get a person clever and immature enough to take advantage of the situation. Use good judgment. I've rarely heard complaints about youth room monitors—probably because sleeping and showering are about all that takes place in hotel rooms.

Hotel Rooms Are Bedrooms

Because hotel rooms are basically bedrooms, I tell the kids they'll not share them with persons of the opposite sex. To spell it out even more clearly I say, no boys in girls' rooms, and no girls in boys' rooms—period!

At home, youths visit each others' bedrooms, close doors, and socialize for hours without so much as a hint of illicit behavior. Frankly, this still bothers me. Bedrooms carry a certain connotation for my generation. I don't feel it's appropriate to get too comfortable with the opposite sex in a bedroom. Kids sometimes don't understand when I put my foot down at this point on trips. Although I'd probably bend on this rule if I just had to answer to youths, the truth is, I answer to their parents. So I don't bend.

This rule has side benefits, however, that ease the sting of restriction for the kids. The boys and girls can relax, knowing they have gender privacy in their rooms. All are free to shower when they feel like it, walk around in various stages of undress, leave unmentionables in full view, and never worry about encountering a surprise guest when they come out of the bath. Another benefit of the same-sex visitors rule is that anyone can get ready for bed, roll over, pull up the covers, and go to sleep without feeling pressured to stay awake to accommodate late-night visitors who hang around too long.

The Gathering Room

Keeping youths out of each others' bedrooms makes sense; but where do they go to talk and watch a movie together? Though not a cheap option, many groups rent an extra hotel room to be used for coed socializing. Spreading the cost of the "gathering room" over the entire group makes this feasible. If your group stays at one location for several days, a gathering room is especially helpful. If you're traveling to a new location each day, save the rental of the gathering room for the last night, when everyone transitions into a lock-in mentality. A gathering room helps control the experience without having to deny the troops.

In the gathering room the youths play cards, watch movies, play guitars, snack, or hang out together. In the absence of a gathering room, youths find other places to hang out together. This is when the desk clerk starts getting calls about a noisy bunch of kids. Even with a gathering room kids need a set of standing rules something like the following:

- The door is never closed.
- The noise must never bother other guests.
- When curfew is reached, the room is no longer available.
- No sleeping is allowed. The group is responsible for waking

youths that may fall asleep and helping them to their private rooms.

- Reclining on the bed with persons of the opposite sex is tolerated—to a point. After all it's the softest seat in the house. Kids are welcome to carve out a spot to watch a movie, but cuddling with that special someone is not allowed. Cuddling sends the wrong message to the rest of the group, and when it gets back home it sounds a lot worse than it actually was.

The gathering room also serves for brief meetings of the whole group or for the evening adult check-in to review the day and go over plans for the next. Providing this room cuts down on hallway gatherings in which groups of youth block the paths of other patrons. It eliminates the excuse for twosomes to hide in stairwells to "talk." Appoint at least one non-driving adult to manage the gathering room and see that it's vacated at curfew.

Curfews

Early curfews on the way to your destination save strength and energy for what's ahead. If the pool closes at 10:00 p.m., for example, all travelers on an outgoing trip should be in their rooms or in the gathering room by 10:00. Empty the gathering room by 11:30, and call for lights out in the rooms by midnight. Coming home the kids can handle a 12:30 or 1:00 a.m. bedtime.

Veteran crews have earned a chance to suggest a curfew along with their rationale for their suggestion. Consider their input. Assigning an adult to each room simplifies enforcing curfew.

In-Room Pay Television

Many motels offer dozens of recent movie titles (rated from G to R) for a pay-per-view cost of $6 per movie, which is added to the room bill. By flipping a few switches, the desk clerk can limit what movies can be rented or even previewed on the basis of their rating. I always ask that they cut X-rated movies. Some youth workers also cut the R-rated movies. Whatever your policy, arrange for the limitations at check-in, prior to giving out keys to the kids.

Room Charges

Reminding the kids about additional room charges only takes a minute, but the first time it isn't done, there's trouble. Additional room charges are billed per room. Any phone call—even for pizza at midnight—can cost money. Youths making long distance calls must call collect or use a credit card. No phone calls are to be charged to the room. Warn them that room service is expensive and the food is often mediocre. And while in-room movies are not expensive, they do add up. Caution them not to preview a movie for too long a time—they may be automatically billed. Collect in cash from occupants all extra charges to their room prior to checking out of the hotel.

Many hotels cut off phones to vacant rooms. A period of up to twenty-minutes can go by between checking in at the front desk and receiving phone service. Since most people try to call home as soon as they drop their luggage on the bed, a dead phone is very frustrating. Find out your hotel's policy from the desk clerk, and if necessary warn the group to wait a few minutes before calling. Also urge the desk to take care of it as soon as possible.

Checking Out

Break the checking-out process into bite-sized pieces to streamline this moment of confusion. Clear communication also helps. Tell the kids something like the following:

- 9:45 — Meet downstairs with luggage in tow.
- 9:50 — Entire group turns in keys. Each room group antes up its room charges.
- 9:55 — Carry luggage to the vehicles.
- 10:00 — Meet on the side lawn for a brief devotion and daily orientation
- 10:10 — Load the luggage into vehicles.
- 10:15 — Pull out of the parking lot.

It's Not a Resort

Don't treat hotels as resorts at which kids check in at 3:00 p.m. and then must keep themselves entertained for the remainder of the day. Hotels are mainly a place to get a good night's rest. Plan activities for your group. Don't arrive too early or stay too long if there's not much to do. Groups just passing through ought to get to the lodging with just enough time to take a dip in the pool, catch the evening news, and get a good night's rest. Pull out in the morning early enough to beat rush hour traffic.

The only motel experience most youth have is vacationing with their folks. The excitement of a motel with friends instead of Mom and Dad usually sets off a normal rambunctiousness in kids. Clear guidelines and sensible rules allow the nights to remain spirited and fun—even for the night clerk and the security guard.

Dealing with Discipline

A few trippers (or one) occasionally make it difficult for everyone else in ways the group should not be expected to handle. I'm talking about insistent use of drugs or alcohol, major fighting, or blatant violations of rules. Ideally youths and adults in a group agree about admissible and inadmissible behavior. Everyone then measures behavior according to these clear guidelines and acts appropriately. We know, however, few things are ideal. One way you can set points of reference for discipline is to involve the entire group in creating a group covenant.

Covenant Building

To establish guidelines for a group covenant the group must know what values it stands for. One camp leader in Georgia takes time before each event to help his kids in defining their shared vision of what the trip is about before creating a covenant for the duration of the trip. Each participant lists three responses on a card: What do I expect from the adults? What do I expect from my peers? What am I willing to put into this trip for making it successful? Each response is discussed by the whole group in three passes around the circle. Then, with good input and expectations fresh in their minds, they draft a covenant. Through the covenant-making process, the travelers also build agreement regarding the goals they hope to achieve through the event.

In addition to clarifying goals, covenants sensitize travelers to specific trip objectives, like behaving toward each other with respect and trust. A trip goal might be to spend two hours each day in silent reflection; a sensitizing objective might address how we believe Christians must behave toward property and resources. Going beyond goal setting to designing specific behavioral rules with specific consequences for breaking them can get out of hand, though. Often the more specific the wording, the more legalistic and heavy-handed the discipline. Page after page of specifics may even encourage some youths to act out simply to show how clever they can be in getting around the rule. Rules and consequences, if included, should be few and stated positively.

Everyone signs the completed covenant to show consent. People who share in the establishment of expectations are more likely to comply with the rules. Depending on how often your group travels and the group turnover, the covenant may be reusable. Before each outing, however, to remind kids of the agreements they're making, review the covenant and have participants sign it.

Point of Diminishing Returns

One way to evaluate appropriate discipline for a youth or group of youths is the notion of the point of diminishing returns. In the financial realm it works like this. Mr. Smith is good at earning lots of money and finally must hire someone else to help manage it. When paying all his employees starts to cost more money than he's making, however, Mr. Smith has reached a point of diminishing returns. What he's getting out of the situation isn't worth what he puts in. At that point he'll fire a few people and put his business back in balance.

Obsessive exercise also demonstrates the point of diminishing returns. Say that Miss Jones runs a few laps daily to shape up. Seeing good results, she ups her number of laps, rising earlier to get them in, and running harder to beat her time. The constant impact, however, causes shin splints. Her knees and feet begin aching all the time. If she continues, she'll be in worse shape than when she wasn't running at all. She has reached a point of diminishing returns.

Now let's apply this notion to group life. God created us to be in community. Being in community requires sensitivity, persistence, and humor to make it work. To sustain a community we must assume that the group has rights that are more important than any one individual's rights. In a Christian community we add the ingredient of servanthood. Youth trips are excellent opportunities to practice skills for being in community. Moving young believers into mature faith in a loving Christian arena is the objective of many trips. That means the more mature kids have to tolerate less mature ones while continuing to model mature behavior.

Once in a while, however, a kid who tests the limits of community building joins the program. As long as the bulk of the youths still attend and still grow, it's okay; helping kids grow is why we have programs in the first place. But when youths stop coming because of the few that sneak out, lie to the leaders, smoke, or fight, it's time to evaluate the return on the investment of time and love in the immature kids. When you hear things like "I can stay at home with my sisters and brothers if I want to put up with insults," you know it's time to deal with the troublemakers. A non-existent youth group helps no one.

Dialogue or Deportation

What do you do when someone on a trip continually violates agreed upon standards and threatens the life of the group? Sending a kid home is extreme. Of the dozens of youth leaders and trip veterans I've consulted, none have sent home more than one or two kids in their entire ministries. They recommend dealing with unacceptable behavior on site.

Meet with the entire group and without singling out or naming names allow kids indulging in problem behavior to make one of the following choices, and expect their verbal response to your face within a specified time.

- To refrain from the problem behavior from this point on.
- To discuss the behavior with the group or with an adult.
- To refuse to stop the behavior, in which case arrangements are made for their departure (or less radical remedy of your choosing).
- To say nothing, in which case arrangements are made for their departure (or less radical remedy of your choosing).
- To say one thing and do another, in which case arrangements are made for their departure (or less radical remedy of your choosing).

Once they've chosen to stop the behavior, drop the issue as if you fully expect them to follow through with their decision. Believe in them and support their good decision. This model lets youths experience the process of making a choice to be in or out of a community, according to the standards the entire group agreed to maintain. No one kicks them out; they reveal by their own choice whether they will or won't work with the group. With calm, clear intent, you treat kids as adults, giving them the opportunity to respond as adults. Their answer lets you judge the importance of problems, how to handle them, and how to know when problems have become significant enough to warrant anything as radical as sending kids home.

Honestly assess whether or not the covenant or the program has been truly violated before setting out the above choices. Ask yourself if you're reacting out of your own insecurity or if someone hit your pet peeve or if you simply lack the ability to cope with a certain behavior. If any of these are the case, it's unfair to transfer *your* problem to individuals or the group as a whole.

Regardless of your view of discipline or the model you use, never get caught bluffing. Leaders who say, "I'll just die if any of you have dirty magazines in the back of that bus," had better die if they do. If you threaten that anyone caught out of their rooms after curfew must call home to request their parents to pay for their immediate return trip, you'd better stick to it. When the president of your group is caught outside after curfew because she wanted to take a walk and think about her Christian commitment, she'd better get on the phone. If you don't follow through, your word will never be trusted—and it will be your own fault.

On the other hand, carefully established consequences or restitutions that are carried out can build up a group. Threats are tricky and often ineffective, but if you must, threaten something you can stick to.

Discipline with Grace

Your grace and maturity while disciplining youths begets grace and maturity in your kids. Those youths who continue to challenge the orders of the group make their own choice to stay or leave. Use grace and maturity. Allow choice and consequences.

Discipline isn't a matter of steps and clever techniques, but an attitude of confidence in yourself and your kids. When something isn't working, find out why before you deal with it. When you know why, offer clear dignified adult choices, and stand with the agreements made from that point.

Part Four

FINISH LINE

When coming in from a long trip, I can smell home. I have to fight the tendency to accelerate the van to eat up the last thirty miles. Home! My own bed, hot water I don't have to share, peace and quiet at mealtime. Before going home, however, I have to face the parking lot.

A few parents are always in the parking lot when we arrive—even if we're two hours early. Their children are gone as soon as they locate their luggage. Then I take stock of the situation—a littered van floor and a parking lot scattered with apparently forgotten luggage, bags, shoes, and more. Getting to work right away, I put leftover luggage in the office, sweep out the vans, empty the glove compartment of trip receipts, and lock up the building. Just as I'm ready to head for my own cozy home, out pop two or three youths who are still waiting for their rides. (Where were these kids while I was doing all the work?)

They don't get picked up for what seems like hours, while I sit, waiting, thinking, and wishing. Sound familiar?

This section can help you avoid this scene as well as give you tips on evaluating your trip, keeping trip records, and managing public relations.

Cleaning Up

For years I struggled with the problem of cleanup after the caravan pulled into home. It wasn't that I didn't know what to do; I just didn't want to do it. Once when I was lamenting how I was too tired to deal with cleanup, a mother set me straight. She said the reason I couldn't summon the energy for cleanup was because I didn't include it as part of my mental picture of the trip experience.

She had a point. I always had plenty of energy for every other aspect of the excursion—departure, journey, arrival, program, the journey back. I started out the trip visualizing the whole journey, right? It's just that my mental picture never went any farther than the pouring out of bodies and gear onto the asphalt. Because that's how I programmed my mind, that's how my body responded. This mother suggested I include final details in my preplanning—cleaning up, waiting with youths whose rides were late, and even the first half hour of being back with my family. After that if I wanted to fall apart, I could.

Preparing for the next outing, I focused my mental picture of the trip from departure through and including cleanup, waiting around, driving to my own home, sharing a few stories, right up to my own private hot shower. It worked.

When I got to the parking lot, I stayed right on task with my energy level high. I enjoyed greeting parents, and waiting with youths became a small extension of the journey—still playing, laughing enthusiastically. I was still up when I greeted my family. After a few moments I began to unwind in the comfort of my own home.

My wife was so excited when I told her about this new approach that she suggested I take it one step further by staying pumped up until I unpacked and put away my gear. Normally I left my bags about three steps inside the door for several days before I was energized enough to deal with unpacking. So I added putting my gear where it belonged to my pre-trip mental picture. I found it was easy to do whatever steps I programmed into my picture of the complete trip.

Once I had a handle on this bit of psychology, I began transferring it to the youths. I'd talk about cleaning up and unpacking at home as if it were still part of the journey. It's helped, I know—I asked their moms. Along with this basic psychological ploy, other measures assist travelers to get home neatly and quickly.

Codependents No More

Upon arriving home after a trip, the twenty/eighty rule strikes again—twenty percent of the people do eighty percent of the work and eighty percent do only twenty percent of the work. A typical pattern starts like this: I announce, "Everyone help clean out the vans. Get the luggage out and set it to the side—carefully, please." The twenty percent get right on it. The eighty percent vie for most original excuse—"I have to go to the bathroom. Can you open the building?" "I need to call my parents to come and pick me up. Can I use the phone?" "I'm late for soccer practice. If I hurry I can still make it. Can I get my stuff and go?" "My parents have been waiting twenty minutes already. Can I go?"

As long as the leader allows it, the twenty/eighty rule remains in effect. The twenty percent continue to bail out the others. Today's catchword for this behavior is *rescuing*, or *codependency*. To lead the way out of this cycle, the twenty percent must stop rescuing. Here's some ways you can gently break the cycle.

☑ *Call a quick meeting* in your office when you arrive home. Invite only those youths you've noticed are among the twenty percent. Leave the rest of the group unpacking. The natural consequence if no one works is that the luggage stays packed until someone does. It makes the point with the eighty percent—they need to work, too.

☑ *Burying the keys* to your office in the bottom of your last piece of community gear can be the needed prod. Only when that last piece of equipment is carried into the proper room can the keys be retrieved and the phoning begin.

☑ *Delay parent pickup* by letting drivers know ahead of time that you consider cleanup to be part of the trip. Parents should wait thirty minutes after receiving a call from youths before leaving to pick them up. Parents informed ahead of time about the purpose of the delay respect it. Now you have enough youths to make quick work of what needs doing. Ask those youths who have cars waiting in the lot for their return to do a specific task prior to their leaving. Kids who drive themselves home usually take with them as many other youths as they can squeeze into the car—and there goes your work force.

Do all this with good natured seriousness. While the kids see through the obvious manipulations, they also learn to recognize that everyone needs to help until everything is done. Slackers know dozens of clever ways to get the more ambitious twenty percent to take care of them. The sooner they see that many hands make light work, the more healthy the group will be.

Lost and Found Bin

Before leaving on a trip, place in your office a big box that can hold all equipment unclaimed at the end of a trip—there's always some. For the next few weeks this box should show up where youths can paw through it to pull out lost items. Parents enjoy going through this box as well. After a few weeks, whatever remains in the box needs a new home. Leftover quality stuff "sells" well at a year-end auction. Instead of bidding with money, youths and parents bid with service hours to be performed by the forgetful offspring.

With a little mind power, some basic psychology, and cooperation with parents, end-of-trip clean-up drudgery can be overcome. Communicate to parents and teens the need for teamwork, explain your working plan to them, stop being a rescuer, and allow your kids the dignity of knowing they carried their weight all the way.

Evaluating Your Trip

22

Chapter

I've heard that experience is not the best teacher, evaluation is.

I'll never forget taking a large truck filled with supplies on a mission trip. I thought I'd driven every kind of vehicle there was—this truck's double axle transmission didn't worry me. I looked at that gear shift, with its little red knob attached to the stick, and figured I'd catch on easily enough. I drove the truck for five days before I was even close to getting it smooth.

I learned that the little red knob makes a six-speed transmission into a twelve speed. The trick to accessing all the speeds is double clutching—using the gas pedal on upshifts, clutching on the down shifts, and operating that red knob in the right sequence so the truck moves forward in a nice and easy progression. Unfortunately, it wasn't my cumulative miles of experience that led me to figure that out. In an idle moment at a gas stop my eyes wandered to a bold sticker right over the driver's door—on it were written clear guidelines for shifting smoothly.

Wouldn't it be nice if we could learn exactly what to do to smooth out our tripping by reading simple instructions posted nearby? Alas, no one set of specific directions could ever give all groups absolute guidance. Each group is unique and each adventure is different, calling for a customized direction sheet. The best source of specific, tailored tips for our future trips are evaluations of past excursions.

Evaluating the Nuts and Bolts

While I encourage you to evaluate your entire event, programs as well as the journey, the following sample questionnaire relates only to the scope of this book—the nuts and bolts of youth group travel.

Trip Evaluation

DESTINATION:
TRIP DATES:

Departure

1. The group departed for this trip as quickly and smoothly as is possible.

     AGREE   1   2   3   4   DISAGREE (circle one)

Please explain your answer.

2. Leaving on this trip is best described as

     CHAOS   1   2   3   4   CONTROL (circle one)

Please explain your answer.

3. List two things you think helped the group depart home smoothly.

4. List two things you feel hindered the group's smooth departure from home.

5. List your recommendations to the planning team on how departures for events could be handled more efficiently.

6. Describe one of the things you'd like to see us do when we're getting ready to leave on a trip.

Community Building

1. List what you feel was most enjoyable about riding in the _____ while on the trip.

2. List what you feel was least enjoyable about riding in the _____ while on this trip.

3. Traveling for hours poses a number of both opportunities and headaches. Please rate the following statements. Explain your answer in the space below each scale.

I tried to get to know some new people this trip.
DEFINITELY　　1　　2　　3　　4　　NO WAY

I tried to get to know some new people on this trip but felt that, to a certain degree, I was rejected.
DEFINITELY　　1　　2　　3　　4　　NO WAY

I enjoyed the games that helped us move around in the vehicles and spend time with different people.
DEFINITELY　　1　　2　　3　　4　　NO WAY

I would rather not play games that force us to spend time with different people while traveling.
DEFINITELY　　1　　2　　3　　4　　NO WAY

Any problems I experienced were normal and not excessive.
DEFINITELY　　1　　2　　3　　4　　NO WAY

As a result of this trip, I feel more comfortable with this group of people than I did when we left home.
DEFINITELY　　1　　2　　3　　4　　NO WAY

I would welcome the opportunity to travel with this group again.
DEFINITELY　　1　　2　　3　　4　　NO WAY

Lodging

1. Please comment on each night's lodging with a score and a brief explanation.

    Friday at the _____

                               GREAT   1   2   3   4   LOUSY

    Comments:

    Saturday at the _____

                               GREAT   1   2   3   4   LOUSY

    Comments:

    Sunday at the _____

                               GREAT   1   2   3   4   LOUSY

    Comments:

Monday at the (and so on) . . .

2. Circle the following statement that best describes your opinion about lodging conditions and cost:
    > Sleep cheaper and save cash.
    > Spend a little more and upgrade the accommodations.
    > Keep it just like it was.
    > > Why?

Food

1. Many consider *good road food* to be an oxymoron. What did you dislike the most about meals while en route?

2. Which "eats" did you like the best?

3. Would you rather eat better food at slower restaurants (knowing it means less time at the destination), or are you satisfied with fast food and getting where you're going sooner?

4. Do you believe buying your own food is the best way to handle meals?

   YES   1   2   3   4   NO

   Explain why or why not:

5. Do you believe prepurchased meals prepared along the way is the best way to handle meals?

   YES   1   2   3   4   NO

   Explain why or why not:

6. What would make mealtimes easier or more convenient?

7. Which one group meal do you wish you had missed?

8. How can we improve group food for the next trip?

Timing and Schedule

1. Each day we traveled a different number of hours. Please answer the following questions about time in the saddle and comment when appropriate.

    Day one: Home to _____ :

                LEAVE EARLIER   1   2   3   4   LEAVE LATER

    Comments:

    Day Two: _____ to _____ :

                LEAVE EARLIER   1   2   3   4   LEAVE LATER

    Comments:

2. Circle your opinion of the number of stops taken.

    Too many   Not enough   Just right

Authority and Discipline

1. Before leaving, the group formulated the rules we agreed to live by on this trip.

    Which ones were most helpful?

    Which ones did you find most difficult?

    Which ones seemed to be unnecessary?

    Looking back on the trip, which ones do you wish we had added?

2. Please comment on the rules we lived by during this event.

    What would you change?

    What would you keep the same?

Valuable Feedback

The preceding questions provide a feel for what a written evaluation can accomplish. Keep in mind the age of your audience as you word your questions, however. Evaluations shouldn't be viewed as a measure of popularity. Many teams reviewing evaluations look only for compliments and positive emotional feedback. Of course, who wouldn't rather read admiring responses than abusive ones? Evaluations do more than reveal or confirm the mood of a given trip. Well-constructed questionnaires assist trippers to make qualitative suggestions, bring out procedural concerns, and write down insights while the trip is still fresh in their memories. The information goes well beyond the popularity ratings. Don't put the forms aside after a casual review of the answers. Thoroughly review your evaluations, and take the comments seriously.

Saving Your Forms

23

Chapter

They say it's easier to do something than to explain why it wasn't done. In tripping it's easier to keep files with pertinent information than to start your next trip dredging your memory for what you did on the last trip. The most helpful files to keep are listed in this chapter to prime you to create files that serve your unique needs.

Health Forms

As soon as you start unpacking, health forms—ever-present during the event—too often disappear. Experienced trippers learn to file health forms alphabetically for use on other trips. Especially in summer when the group takes frequent day trips, parents tire of writing out insurance numbers and health histories for their children. Keeping health forms on file means parents only need to sign a medical release dated for each new event.

The forms are not filed indefinitely, however. Each year parents should update them—perhaps at the beginning of the summer, or whenever your group's heavy trip time occurs. Although keeping this file current can be tedious for you, it's an appreciated courtesy to the parents of your kids.

Trip Sheets

If you must record mileage and other details regarding the trip vehicles, do it before you lock up at the end of a trip. Record the odometer reading. Evaluate the apparent condition of the vehicle, and comment about what might have been damaged or broken. Record the drivers' names and license numbers. Then put the form in the proper staff member's box before heading home to family and food.

These sheets are the bane of my existence. While I often wonder what purpose they serve, I've learned that not filling them out isn't the way to protest their use. Follow through with trip responsibilities to the bitter end, and you'll sleep better not anticipating hurrying around the next morning on an event that's history.

Finances

Counting money, putting receipts in order, listing where, how, and how much money was used is the one aspect of tripping that shouldn't be done in the twilight of an event when the mind isn't sharp and focused. Within a day or two of completing an event is soon enough, but don't put it off any longer. White receipts, even with notes on them, lose their context after a few weeks. Do your accounting while your mind is close enough to the event to make a clear and accurate report of how cash was handled. Some churches want a line-by-line breakdown of every expense on a trip; others are happy with a balance sheet showing how much cash was taken, how much was actually used, and what happened to the difference. Still others don't ask for any report at all. (But beware. Perhaps no one asked for a report because no one had a problem with anything—at the time. As soon as a problem emerges, however, suddenly everyone wants facts. If only for your peace of mind, keep close track of the money.)

Insurance Forms and Claims

Any incident that required medical care must be followed up with phone calls to the agents who wrote the affected policies. Report what happened, ask questions about what else needs to be done, and then do it. Emergency room bills can get real ugly. A hospital attacks the credit of whomever signed the report when treatment was administrated—most likely you. Call, check it out, call again. Let people know bills are coming, reports are pending, and that money will be paid. This hassle is preferable to what can happen if you don't follow up.

Just Do It

These final trip details are difficult steps, easy to put off, and most likely to be a thorn in the side later. Your procrastination can empower these details to tear at the fabric of an otherwise great outing. Just do it!

Sharing the Good News

24

Chapter

D ave worked hard to offer good youth programs, challenging events, and meaningful adventures. A humble person, comfortable with his ego, Dave wasn't interested in developing a name for himself or blowing his own horn. After a summer of service projects, a spiritual life retreat, Bible studies, and weekly evening programs, he was certain his youth group would have its best attendance ever in the autumn.

It almost never happened.

Just before his fall kick-off event, he overheard some of the church folks in a conversation something like this: "I hear we might be looking for a new youth leader. I wish we had one that did more things with the youths. They should be doing service projects, spiritual life retreats, Bible studies, and offering weekly evening programs."

Public Relations: A Fact of Life

Youth workers send messages whether they intend to or not. Each time people hear about an event before the fact, after it's over, or never, they receive a message. Youth workers holding long-term positions are typically those who have accepted the reality of working public relations in favor of the group. The following sampler of ways other youth workers tackle public relations is meant to move you to take seriously the need to do something—anything—to let parents and others know what happened on your trip. Good public relations is vital to the steady growth and success not only of your youth trips, but of your whole youth ministry.

Slides

One of the most versatile and effective methods to present significant parts of a journey is by slides. For one thing, taking slide pictures is easy. A youth worker in Arkansas, for example, gives all youths in the group with a camera, a roll of slide film to use at their discretion. Slide film isn't expensive to buy or develop, and when all the developed slides are sorted and arranged, they make a wonderful chronological show. Slides that don't fit the story, or turn out poorly, can be set aside.

Availability is another asset of this medium. Almost every gift shop or tourist haven carries a sleeve of ready-made slides for purchasing. These professional shots show the area sights in the best light. Even special effect sleeves can be purchased. I once found a sleeve of sunset slides in Colorado. I purchased them to use as ending slides for many different shows. A Florida youth worker wanted to create her own special effect. She sent the vehicles in her caravan driving off into a sunset while she stayed along the side of the road taking photos. They then turned around and picked her up. It made a great last slide for the show.

Youth workers agree, however, that the best slides and the best shows focus on the people in the group. Slides of mountains, streams, or neighborhoods get yawns. Parents like to see their children in the setting; youths like to see themselves as they were on the adventure. People pictures are the key to great public relations photos.

Selecting a theme gives the final show direction. Some themes are suggested by the kinds of pictures that turn out well. Maybe the group shots showing the kids in specific settings—in front of city limits signs, the orphanage, the house they painted—tell the story best. Or maybe the candid shots the group took of each other lead you to create "a day in the life" of the trippers, showing every facet of the youths' daily life during the event—from waking to sleeping.

Music gives direction to your show. I saw a youth group present a slide show of its summer mission project to the song "I've Got My Mind Set On You" by George Harrison. This song talks about focusing on one thing, how much time it takes, how much money it takes, and so forth, without ever identifying the object of all this attention. This group suggested the focus via pictures of its missions event. The object the kids set their minds on was the group of people they worked with. The need for money was paired with slides of fundraisers. The overall effect was fantastic.

Using a script is another way to provide a theme for a show. Try putting the event into the frame of a passage of Scripture. Read the written script as you present the show, frame by frame.

A slide show is effective—up to a point. Generally, any slide show lasting more than fifteen minutes should be pared down. Too often long shows outlast the interest of the audience. One youth worker suggests putting all the unused slides into another carousel and showing them after the conclusion of the actual presentation for those who want to hang around to see pictures of the kids. Terribly unflattering slides should be held out or destroyed, however.

A slide show can track the group's history, encourage other youths to attend future events, and assist board members to understand why money needs to be provided. Let me say, however, that the shows that most motivate adults to support your trips are those picturing youths taking advantage of opportunities to grow in their faith. Opportunities for and evidence of spiritual growth should be presented no matter what the theme of the show. This is what parents and other adults hope characterizes trips. Keep Christ at the center of the presentation, and people will continue to entrust their children to your events.

Community Journal with a Theme

A variation of the community journal (chapter 12) is to journal with a theme. Say 1 Corinthians 13 is the chosen theme for a community journal. All youths study that chapter, familiarize themselves with the words of Paul, then rewrite the chapter in their own words. Then each day of the journey, as many kids as possible write in the community journal their reflections on different aspects of that passage, relating it to what happened that day. They may retell an incident when they saw selfless love played out, how some of their own childish ways yielded to more mature ones, and so on.

Share the journal with the church by editing the whole thing, culling out the best thoughts and insights for a shared reading. Or photocopy parts or the whole thing to offer as the group's written statement of the growth and insight they retained from the trip. Even the youngest kids can come up with insights that surprise us.

Video

A video is a magical record of a trip that can be shown for years. Nothing matches the response of seniors viewing a video featuring them on a junior high trip.

The youths enjoy being captured on tape as well as making a creatively taped trip journal. Cameras are expensive toys and require education and gentle handling.

Few video recordings are shot well enough to view without editing, however. Although anyone with two VCRs can do rough editing, a good job requires using special equipment that's expensive to access. Quality editing takes time and experience. But depending on your purpose for the finished product, a well-edited video may be worth it—and it can be duplicated for all the trippers.

Tact and taste need to be stressed to budding filmmakers. Kids can do far better than merely to check out the tonsils of screaming youths as they run up to the camera. School them in an underlying mind-set of building each other up and uniting the group, rather than embarrassing people or dividing the group. Unity and community building are the filters through which all activities should be screened.

Songs and Stories

Allowing the kids to discover their own way to tell the story of their trip—through skits, drama, original songs, plays, individuals telling anecdotes on themselves—is almost always more meaningful and effective to the tellers and the hearers than if you prepare a tidy presentation. Having the youths themselves present the show is the best way to go whenever possible.

Written Accounts

Groups without a forum to share about a trip may consider writing out their experiences. Many organizations publish a periodic newsletter or magazine that may print a well-written contribution. Newspapers sometimes use feature stories with quality black-and-white photographs. Sunday papers often highlight various groups whose activities are worthy of note. A one-page summary can be printed and distributed at various meetings or classes that don't require verbal or visual support.

Written accounts can effectively promote the goals of your trip and help parents to understand what you accomplished. The kids' written trip summaries can also serve as an excellent tool for evaluation. Putting their thoughts into writing challenges them to look beyond mere facts about where they went and what they did to examine their perceptions of the purposes of the trip.

Planting Seeds for the Future

Whenever you create an effective public relations piece, don't overlook the opportunity to answer the question, what next? If the kids have made accomplishments and if their good experience has been conveyed, you've opened a window of opportunity for a brief moment. Your parents and supervisors are ready to hear what the next step is—what finances, time investment, leadership, and equipment are needed for the next trip. They want to hear how the next trip fits into your church's long-range goals. Think of this experience as planting seeds, though, not harvesting. Scatter ideas for the future—plans with enough shape to assure hearers that you plan ahead well, but not so much that they feel their support is taken for granted. Let them know they'll be consulted as the plan unfolds. Then in following weeks and months, keep the idea alive in parents and supervisors, without nagging. Planting seeds isn't manipulation; it's solid administrative work. The best time to plant seeds is right after people have seen how effective a previous experience has been. Nurture them with details as times goes on. Ideas with merit come up, grow, and produce a crop. No one time schedule covers the rate at which seed ideas mature—some grow quickly and easily, while others take a long time and require tedious labor. Unfortunately, some ideas don't make it regardless of how long they are worked.

Closing the Circle

As seeds of new trip ideas are planted and grow, a new process of bringing parents and youths into the directing and shaping of an idea begins. Even though that's where this book began, the tripping process has no clear-cut beginning. A group trip is an evolving cycle of dreams, seeding, nurturing, harvesting, sharing the fruits of the labor, and dreaming new dreams.

Happy trails!

APPENDIX

Condos and Resorts

Call the Chamber of Commerce or the Visitors and Convention Bureau of the site you hope to visit and ask for phone numbers of local motels, condo management companies, and local realtors. It's normal to get several phone numbers; call them all. Be patient. In nearly every city I've been, there was a management company who would work with me.

You can also call the National Interim Housing Network (1-800-742-6446). This group has information on available condos nationwide. Many affiliates of the network cater only to families moving to new cities, but not all of them. It's always worth checking.

Whichever resource you contact, conduct your conversation from a prepared list of questions and jot down the information you receive beside the questions. Here are some questions you need to ask.

1. What is the name of the person on the phone? (Stick with that person each time you call back.)
2. Do they handle groups?
3. Are accommodations available for your dates?

4. How many individuals can sleep in a unit?
5. What are their rates—daily, weekly, or monthly? Do they offer multiple-unit discounts?
6. What is the total cost for the stay? Multiply the rate per unit ($150) by the number of nights (three) times the number of units needed (five). That's $150 x 3 x 5 = $2,250. Use that figure in all the following discussions. After all, which vision is more appealing to a management company: dozens of screaming youths, or $2,250 dollars in their coffers? No contest. Get the biggest dollar amount you can muster into the conversation as soon as possible. Money talks.
7. Get pertinent phone numbers, ask if an 800 number is available. Tell them you'll call again after some serious number crunching is done.

When you've narrowed your choices to two or three, begin your call backs. Share with managers what you have discovered. Let them know they are a top choice, and ask them for the best deal they can manage. Be gracious about it. Then continue your questioning.

8. Will linens and towels be provided? Is there a cleaning charge for using them? (If there is and it's high, consider having your kids bring sleeping bags and their own towels.)
9. What is the kitchen equipped with? Does it have a microwave?
10. How late is the pool open? What other recreation possibilities are available? Do they charge a fee to use them? Is equipment available for rent? What kinds? How much?

11. What kind of a deposit is necessary? When is it due? Is it refund-able? When is it paid back? (A note here on damage deposits. Request a walk-through upon arrival and again at checkout. A walk-through protects you from difficult-to-resolve claims filed weeks after you've returned home. Without a walk-through, it's your word against theirs.)
12. What are your payment options—cash, check, or credit card?
13. When are the quiet hours?
14. What security exists?
15. Can you have a cookout?
16. Is there a meeting area available? Does it cost extra? What equipment is available (VCR, monitor, overhead projector, sound system, podium, chalkboard)?
17. Are there other specific house rules that you should know of?

Motels and Hotels

To ask the right questions, you'll need know if the group is staying one night or several and if you'll arrive early enough to take advantage of amenities. If your group plans to arrive at 11:00 p.m. and leave again at 7:00 a.m., for example, they need little more than a bed and shower. If you're staying for a few days, the extras become more important. Use the following list of extras to spark questions about what your group really needs in a place to stay.

A block of rooms apart from other guests
Adjoining rooms
Indoor/Outdoor pool (and its hours)
Whirlpool/Hot tub/Steam room/Sauna/Fitness room

Cable TV
In-room coffee
Continental breakfast
Laundry facilities
Exercise equipment
Restaurant on premises
Game room
Interior access to rooms or exterior?
   (Security is better on interior-accessed rooms.)
Earliest check in/latest checkout
Luggage storage while you visit the sites after checkout
Handicap accessibility
Additional taxes to the bill—bedroom tax, local additional taxes
   (It's not uncommon to pay up to ten percent in some areas.)
Alcohol service on the premises
   (This is generally a big no-no. Where there's a bar, there's drinking. Where there's drinking, there may be inebriation. Where there are inebriated individuals and innocent youths, trouble may be closer than you want to worry about.)

There are two ways to make reservations—calling an 800-number central reservation service (1-800-555-1212) or directly contacting a specific front desk. Clerks at a central reservation desk have no clear picture of what each motel looks like or how to give street directions to the motel. The 800 operators are prepared to quickly give you information about several cities and locations and to quote you chain-wide group rates.

Talking directly to individual motel managers can garner more specific and helpful information. How new is the facility? Newer plants are generally cleaner and better equipped. If the facility isn't new, has it been renovated in the last five years? What is the pool like? Are adjoining rooms available? Is continental breakfast included? Is there room to park a bus?

In all your conversations, be friendly and polite. Motel managers may be skeptical about booking a youth group; don't add to their skepticism with less-than-courteous manners.